SEXUAL CHAOS

SEXUAL CHAOS

The Personal and Social Consequences of the Sexual Revolution

John N. Vertefeuille

CROSSWAY BOOKS • WESTCHESTER, ILLINOIS
A DIVISION OF GOOD NEWS PUBLISHERS

Sexual Chaos. Copyright © 1988 by John N. Vertefeuille. Published by Crossway Books, a division of Good News Publishers, Westchester, Illinois 60153.

First printing, 1988

Printed in the United States of America

Library of Congress Catalog Card Number 87-71891

ISBN 0-89107-430-9

CONTENTS

ACKNOWLEDGMENTS

Very special thanks must go to the following people, without whom this first attempt would surely have been my last:

Howard Flaherty, whose gift is making things happen.

Jan Dennis, who said yes to a first-time author.

Ken Willhite and Eydie Patton, who saved the day for me more than once.

And, of course, my wife Cynthia, who I know believes in me more than I believe in myself.

PART I

UNDERSTANDING THE SEXUAL ORDER

ONE

PURPOSE IN POLARITY

*M*an is male and female. This is perhaps the single most important fact of human society. So much so that the great anthropologist Margaret Mead has said that if any human society is to survive, "it must have a pattern of social life that comes to terms with the differences between the sexes."[1] In fact, to deny the differences between the sexes—in the name of androgyny, homosexuality, women's lib, or some quixotic quest to achieve "true humanity"—denies not only the fulfillment of God's order for the family and society, but denies the greatest and most distinctive proclamation ever made about man—that he is created in the image of God.

But why is sexual differentiation so important? There is, of course, the obvious biological fact which necessitates the differences between the sexes as fundamental for the propagation of the human race. In a very real sense, to deny the differences between the sexes is to deny the future. However, it must be understood that the importance of man's sexual differences is not limited to the function of his anatomy. The polarity between the sexes is more than a biological fact. It is also a theological fact. And if our theology informs the way we live at all, it will become a social and psychological fact as well. Perhaps no other attribute of man so defines who he is as does his maleness and femaleness.

Yet, one of the greatest questions man faces about himself today is whether or not he will allow his sexual differentiation to continue to play its part in defining who he is. While no one disagrees that gender distinctions color almost every aspect of our lives, from the way we dress and raise our children to the way we behave and relate to each other, what is at question today is whether they should color our lives at all. In times past, the distinctions between the sexes were necessary and clearly understood. Men, because of their greater physical strength, were needed as warriors and hunters. Women were left at home to birth and nurture children (preferably boys to replenish the warrior stock and assist with the hunt).

But modern technology has changed all that. In the modern world men are no longer necessary. In an age of sophisticated weaponry physical strength is no longer needed as a warrior; a woman can push a button as well as a man. The same is true of the provider role. And what a woman cannot provide for herself, the government will. Nor is it any longer necessary for the woman to stay at home and birth and nurture her children. The "modern" woman, reluctant to remove herself from a rewarding career, might still produce a child by hiring a surrogate mother to carry her baby to term.[2] The inconvenience of raising the child is given to the day-care center and eventually the public schools. Thus rather than complementing one another, male and female are now competing with each other for survival, and sexual distinctions are minimized.

Now this state of affairs would be of little concern to us if we bought into secular man's ideas about himself. For modern scientific man, sexual differentiation is nothing more than a development of the evolutionary process. Man has been reduced from a complex being in the image of God into a socialized biochemical accident, a product of matter, time and chance. Therefore, how one understands the differences between the sexes is not something that must necessarily remain static. While anatomical sexual distinctions may remain unchanged, the same is not true of gender distinctions (i.e., one's social and psychological understanding of his sexuality).

Since gender distinctions are largely acquired through the process of socialization, they become subject to the discoveries of science and the pronouncements of culture, which are themselves in a constant state of flux and change. Thus, when science developed the birth control pill it revolutionized society's attitudes and behavior toward sex. The woman, liberated from the fear of pregnancy, was able to postpone marriage and family in favor of pursuing her career. The man, released from marriage, became a sexual nomad, aggressively seeking new territories of conquest.

Freed from moral absolutes and biological imperatives, sex was no longer a matter of procreation and expressing love, but a means of recreation. This novel attitude toward sex opened the door to all kinds of sexual experimentation such as multipartner sex, same-sex relations, anonymous sex, and bestiality. Bisexuality, homosexuality, sadomasochism, pedophilia, and other previously forbidden sexual experiences became the new frontiers. The more people experimented, the less gender distinctions mattered. The result has been a society largely confused about its sexual identity and therefore disconnected from any lasting sense of fulfillment in marriage and family. In the wake of this confusion, society is paying a high price. The family continues to disintegrate, threatening the stability of our culture; the decline of population growth depletes our economy of valuable human resources so that the burden of the many rests more and more on the few; a host of sexually transmitted diseases (PID, chlamydia, incurable genital herpes) ravages society; and AIDS moves closer to epidemic proportions every day.

Man can no longer afford to ignore the differences between the sexes and what they mean to his survival. Nor can he any longer seek to understand himself apart from his Designer. Man must recapture what it means to be created in the image of God as *male* and *female*. He must understand that his sexuality does indeed color every aspect of his life. Man must first be understood theologically before he can be understood biologically, psychologically, or socially. If he fails in this quest he will take a path that will ultimately lead to his destruction. And so it is to the Word of God we turn as the basis for understanding the purpose of our sexual polarity.

SEXUAL POLARITY AND THE THEOLOGICAL NATURE OF MAN

The first statement we read about man is neither biological nor social; it is theological:

God said, "Let us make man in our image" (Gen. 1:26). Of all the living creatures created by God, man alone is differentiated as being in the image of God. Whereas the animals are brought forth by the Word of God, man is brought forth by the divine breath of God (cf. Gen. 1:25; 2:7). While it is true that man does share a creatureliness with the animals, he is not merely the highest order on the taxonomical scale of living beings. Man transcends the order of the animals by God's sovereign decree to make man in His own image. But what does it mean for man to be in the image of God?

13

Scripture declares that man is created in the divine image and explicates that in terms of being male and female.

So God created man in his own image, in the image of God he created him; male and female he created them. (Gen. 1:27)

Although traditional theology has always affirmed that men and women are in the divine image, it has largely overlooked the male/female distinction as that in which the image consists.[3] Instead, the image of God has usually been seen in light of what separates him from the animals. Thus, man's moral self-transcendence (the knowledge of right from wrong), his rationality, creativity, and dominion over the created order have set the perimeters of defining the image of God in man. While such attributes are surely a part of what it means to be in the divine image, they ignore the proximity of the Genesis 1:27 statement about the image of God and its connection to the fact that man is created in that image as male and female. If Genesis 1:27b ("male and female he created them") is best understood as an exposition of 1:27a ("in the image of God he created him"), then the first thing it means for man to be in the image of God is that he is male and female. This observation is fundamental to our understanding of man and bears further explanation.

Of course, when we say that man is in the image of God we certainly do not mean that he is an exact replica or duplication of God, but rather that he corresponds to or reflects who God is. Despite the masculine gender pronouns used for God throughout Scripture, we know that He is neither male nor female. Moreover, we also know that God is not corporeal. The Bible teaches that God is spirit. It is, perhaps, the very invisibility of God that has prevented us from thinking that the image of God in man could be seen in anything which pertains to man's physical nature. How can we say that man's physical being, particularly the fact that he is created male and female, reflects anything of the invisible God?

Notice that man is not created in the singular but in the plural: male and female. This is our first important observation of what it means to be in the image of God, for we find that God Himself exists as a plurality of being. In Genesis 1:26 God said, "Let us make man in *our* image. . . ." It has been suggested that the use of

14

"us" is simply a plurality of royalty or a literary plurality of authorship (note the way we have been using the plural "we" in this chapter). But neither of these idioms is familiar to the Hebrew. Moreover, since the Hebrew has no lack for singular words for God, it is best to understand this plural form for what it is—the "us" of plurality.[4] It can be said then that God is a kind of society or fellowship within Himself. God does not exist as a solitary God, but as a Triune God who experiences Himself in terms of relationship—Father, Son and Spirit.[5] While we must make sure that we do not express this relationship as tri-theism, we must nevertheless understand that Father, Son, and Spirit are each differentiated from the other. If, therefore, God exists as a God whose very being is that of a fellowship of persons, then man, who is in His likeness (plural), cannot exist as a solitary man, but as man in fellowship with himself. And the nature of this fellowship is as male and female.

The second creation narrative of Genesis makes the nature of this fellowship more explicit. In Genesis 2:18 God says that it is not good for man to dwell in a state of aloneness. But then, in an interesting juxtaposition of Scripture, the animals are brought to Adam to see what he would call them, as if in the process of doing so it might become apparent to the man that there is none like himself. As Adam names each animal, the differentiation between them is confirmed. There is neither a correspondence between them, nor a response to their being. But when God creates woman and brings her before the man, there is an immediate response (Gen. 2:23). Here is something different from the other creatures. Man encounters something of himself in the woman—"This is now bone of my bone and flesh of my flesh." The woman emerges, not as another individual being, but as the complement to the man—different and yet alike. The state of man's aloneness is thus met, not in the creation of another individual Adam, but in the complementarity of the woman.

It is clear that man is not a solitary creature, but one who is created to be in fellowship. Moreover, this fellowship is not revealed as a fellowship without regard to his sexuality, but is necessarily connected to it. Man is not simply in fellowship with his neighbor; intrinsic to the way in which man is made known to another is the fact that he encounters the other as "he" or "she." He is drawn to the opposite sex in a way that is quite different than the way in which he meets his own sex. The Bible does not say that God created man in his own image as a "you" and "me"; what it does say is that God created man in His own image as *male* and *female*. Thus, the primal form of humanity is rooted in human sexuality; it is fellowship of man and woman.[6] To be sure, human existence is experienced in a multitude of social relations—husband, wife, parent, child, friend—but all these are secondary differentiations. Man is first and always male or female.[7]

Thus far we have observed that God exists as a fellowship differentiated as Father, Son, and Spirit, and that man was created to exist as a fellowship differentiated as male and female. But what must be answered is whether or not the fellowship of man as male and female corresponds in any way to the divine fellowship. The answer to this question will require that we understand something of the nature of the fellowship of God.

While the Bible reveals the fellowship of God in three persons (Father, Son, and Holy Spirit), it is the familial differentiation of God seen through the Incarnation that gives us the best insight into that fellowship. In the concepts "Father" and "Son" we are able to determine that the fellowship of God goes beyond a mere partnership within the Godhead. Above all, the terms "Father" and "Son" denote a complementarity of relationship which becomes determinative of God's action. As Ray Anderson suggests, there is a reciprocal relation between the Father and the Son in which "the Father is consistently revealed as the source of all God wills" and "the Son is revealed as the source of all God is willing to be as perfect response to his own determination."[8] In other words, the Son subordinates His own will to the Father in a complementarity of relationship which functions in perfectly accomplishing the will of God.

Thus, when God desired that men should be saved, there was no divine drawing of straws or heavenly coin-toss between the Father and the pre-existent Son to see who would go. Rather, the Son is sent from the Father to do the will of the Father (John 3:16; 7:16; 8:29; 14:24). This is not to suggest that the subordination of the Son to the Father is limited to salvation history or that it in any way implies inequality, for in seeing the Son one also sees the Father (cf. John 1:1; 14:9).

The issue is not one of equality, but of complementarity. Complementarity must not be understood as inequality but as fulfillment in relation to the other.[9] Thus we find that within the perfect unity of God there is a differentiation within His being which reveals a complementarity in which there is neither an advantage nor disadvantage in the relationship.[10]

Now if the nature of God's fellowship within Himself is expressed as both a differentiation and a complementarity of being, and if there is a correspondence between God and the image of God in man as *male* and *female*, then we expect to find a similar fellowship expressed as a complementarity in the differentiation of the sexes. In regard to this, what might seem to be obvious in the way the sexes differ and complement one another is not always so—at least to those who desire to dismantle traditional sex roles in the name of "sexual equality" (by this is meant that sexual differentiation is of little or no consequence to the family or society). Therefore, we must establish whether there is indeed a differentiation of the sexes and if a complementarity exists within it.

Despite the blather of the sexual liberationists, the two sexes are *not* essentially the same, nor are their roles mutually interchangeable. The differences between the sexes are distinct and profound, rooted in the prenatal beginnings of life. Sexual differentiation begins with chromosomes which determine all genderrelated characteristics of the developing fetus. All eggs have an X chromosome, but the sperm may carry an X or a Y. If the egg is fertilized with an X-bearing chromosome, the resulting XX chromosomal structure will produce a biological female. If the egg is fertilized with a Y-bearing chromosome, the XY chromosome pattern will develop into a biological male.

After six weeks following conception, the fetal gonads will respond to the Y chromosome of a male by becoming testicles; if no Y chromosome is present, the undifferentiated gonads will develop into ovaries. Once the gonads have differentiated into testicles they will begin to manufacture male sex hormones called androgen. In females the sex hormone, estrogen, will be produced. Neuroendocrinologists have shown that these sex hormones have a significant influence on brain development. Obviously, the female brain must be developed to govern such processes as menstruation, gestation, and lactation, whereas the male brain must govern such processes as sperm production and erection of the penis.

Moreover, there is now evidence that sex hormones play a part in influencing our social behavior.[11] During adolescence the hormonal secretion of testosterone in the male will begin to promote

17

greater physical strength and sexual drive. It will also promote competition and aggressive behavior. However, the hormonal administration in the female will bring different kinds of changes. She will begin menstruation, her body will fill out, and she will be reminded of her potential to be wife and mother. From conception to maturity, hormonal influences affect the physical development and psychological temperaments of males and females in different ways.

The males tend to be greater in muscular strength, more aggressive, boisterous, and volatile. He is sexually compulsive, domineering, and tends to validate his manhood through action. He is superior in mathematical ability and visual-spatial skills. The female, on the other hand, is inclined to be more nurturant, domestic, and socially empathetic. She tends to have greater verbal facility and manual dexterity, receives subtle vocal and visual messages more accurately, and is more attentive to sounds and their emotional meanings.

These sexual differences describe not only our anatomical distinctions, but also the terms on which we meet and differentiate one another as persons. Indeed, if sexual differentiation is the carrier of the image of God, it cannot do so at the physical or biological level alone. The image of God as reflected in the polarity of the sexes rests in the potential of human sexuality to bring a differentiation of personhood. Being male or female does not by itself incorporate a differentiation of personhood. The animals also share a differentiation of the sexes, but their instinctual coming together at the biological level does not include a differentiation of being. There is no sense in which animals bring a disclosure of the self to the other or where the mystery of being is encountered in the other. Animals mate, but they do not meet.

Human beings, however, not only mate—they "meet."[12] It is perhaps not without significance that within the animal kingdom man alone mates face to face—not simply in response to an instinctual call to reproduce, but as a freely entered upon encounter of personhood. It is in the *meeting* of the sexes that differentiation of persons occurs. And it is in the meeting of the sexes that a complementarity of relationship occurs which, like the complementarity of God, becomes determinative of action.

The complementarity of the sexes is most obvious again at the physical level. The male has a penis which perfectly complements the female vagina. The action which is determined by this arrangement is the command of God to mate and thereby to be "fruitful and increase in number . . ." (Gen. 1:28). The meeting of persons is thus joined with the mating of persons and gives rise to a social order in which ultimate differentiation is met in ultimate complementarity—the man and woman become one flesh in a permanent commitment to one another (Gen. 2:24). The result is that the will of God is accomplished in the "fruitfulness" of children. In the establishment of this fellowship, God not only reveals His plan for male and female in the created order, but He also reveals something of Himself through them.

It is interesting that the complementarity of God also produces children (cf. Acts 17:29; Rom. 8:14; 2 Cor. 6:18; 1 John 3:1, 2). As God is not a solitary God, but a God in fellowship with Himself as a differentiated being, so man reflects that fellowship in his sexual differentiation as male and female. It is in this differentiation that man encounters the mystery of his person rooted in the complementarity of his being and finds purpose and fulfillment in life.

The theological imperative is clear: If we are to acknowledge the image of God in man, and His purpose for man, we must acknowledge the polarity of the sexes. Moreover, it is the Biblical insistence on maintaining our sexual distinctions which determines the social order.

MARRIAGE—
MANDATE OR OPTION?

*N*othing informs the way we live today as much as how we view tomorrow. It is the future that gives meaning to the present. History, from the Biblical perspective, has a purposeful beginning and a definite end. It begins with the creation of man by God, and moves with direction toward the consummation of man in Christ when time will be no more and eternal life will be enjoyed by those who are in Christ. It is this future hope that enables the Christian to bear his present sufferings and confirms his Christian ethic—for if there is no future hope, the apostle tells us, then "Let us eat and drink, for tomorrow we die" (1 Cor. 15:32).

When history has no purposeful beginning, it has no purposeful end. Disconnect ourselves from the future, and life is left without meaning, hope, or purpose. Freedom from the future leads to a hedonism for today. A culture preoccupied with the present loses its ability to project the future consequences of its present actions because it has lost the larger picture into which it fits. Like a spoiled child, it becomes selfish, demanding and consumptive. A society which loses its commitment to future generations ultimately assigns itself to its own demise.

The health and vitality of a society, therefore, resides in its connectedness to the future. And what connects a society to the future? The answer is children. The survival of society will be determined by whether or not men and women will perform the sexual roles for which they were created—to bear children (Gen. 1:28).

However, abortion-on-demand, disintegrating families, and the decline of marriage tell us that our society is in trouble—for we are pulling the plug that connects us to the future. Our only hope of getting reconnected will be a return to three basic principles: (1) We must accept the command of God for the created order: to "be fruitful and increase in number"—i.e., to bear children (Gen. 1:28). (2) We must accept marriage as the agency through which children are born and nurtured. (3) We must maintain the differences between the sexes as the basis of marriage.

GOD'S COMMAND FOR THE CREATED ORDER

> So God created man in his own image . . . male and female he created them. God blessed them and said to them, "Be fruitful and increase in number; fill the earth and subdue it." (Gen. 1:27, 28)

For the secular man or woman these words are less than palatable and, considering modern man's view of history, understandably so. This is because secular man has rejected an authentic view of history and has replaced it with one of his own.

It seems there are really only two choices concerning man's history. The first is that God created man and woman in His image and laid before them a divinely ordered task—to fill the earth by bearing children and to rule as God's vice-regent over His creation. Man's creation is thus intentional and purposeful.

The second choice is the one articulated in the philosophy of the French molecular biologist and Nobel prize winner Jacques Monod in *Newsweek* magazine:

> . . . man's existence is due to the chance collision between miniscule particles of nucleic acid and proteins in the vast "pre-biotic soup." Indeed . . . all life results from interaction of pure chance. . . .[1]

In this view, man's history has a beginning, although no one is quite sure when; but it certainly isn't intentional. This idea of man's beginning, so widely accepted by secular man, leaves man devoid of understanding what his purpose in life should be and clueless as to what his future holds. Purpose and meaning in life are formed in what man himself can give it.

What are the consequences of these two views for man and society? In the Biblical view, man's existence is given meaning. Because his life is purposeful, his future is purposeful and does not remain a total mystery. His future does not need to be feared but can be welcomed as being in God's sovereign control. He recognizes that he has a reponsibility to future generations and must therefore rule responsibly over creation. Moreover, he is given a template in his sexuality that informs his sociology. Man recognizes that he is distinctly differentiated as male and female in order to fulfill the purpose of God for which he was created. Marriage is not an ill-regarded social option but a means of accomplishing the will of God.

In the evolutionary view man's future is a cause of anxiety. Fully aware of his capacity for self-destruction, man is caught up in a frantic race to save himself from his own future. In essence, he attempts to overcome his fear of the future by working to overcome his own mortality. His own self-defined task is to build an environment which will prolong life indefinitely so that he will no longer need to fear the future—a life that never ends is a life that is ever in the present.

Thus, the ultimate quest of the sciences in the evolutionary model is to prolong human life as long as possible. Medical science works toward the task of eliminating sickness and disease in order to extend life indefinitely. Environmentalists work to protect the resources of the planet in order to extend life. Politicians work to protect men from themselves in order to extend life. Technicians work on preserving food resources in order to extend life.

Central to these concerns is the limitation of population growth. Overpopulation, modernists argue, is a threat to man's resources of food, natural materials, and available living space.

The solution to this seeming threat, of course, is simple: limit the birth of children; or, if need be, eliminate children altogether. This attitude is already being implemented at the personal level. The shrinking family and over a million abortions a year testify to secular man's belief that children are not "an inheritance from the Lord," but a "threat" to one's "personal spaces"—a threat which must be eliminated at all costs, even the cost of life. Such an attitude not only directly contradicts the command of God concerning the taking of life—it also contradicts the command of God concerning the giving of life. Man has been ordained to be fruitful and to fill the earth.

Certainly there are those who will argue that the task is complete, the earth is full, it's time to be "responsible." Indeed, it is always "time" to be responsible, and responsibility requires us to challenge this chatter about overpopulation and the quality of life it is supposedly destroying. While the preachers of zero population growth continue to urge women to abandon the role of wife and mother for the sake of society, the United States has now dropped below the replacement level of reproduction.[2] In other words, we are not producing enough babies in society to replace those members who are dying.

What this means in terms of quality of life is that a rising number of people within the population are the elderly whose burden of support rests on an ever-declining number of younger citizens. As a result, the tax rate rises and workers tend to work less, women bear even fewer children and ultimately society collapses.[3] The irony is superb: by denying children a future for the purpose of saving society we end up destroying the very thing we wanted to save.

Responsibility means living in "response" to the command of God. To be sure, we must continually ask ourselves how this is to be done in a sinful world; but we must never come to a place where we say we are released from God's command to be fruitful. We cannot afford to erase our children from our tomorrow. The children are our future, and we must surely believe that God in His infinite wisdom had a plan to insure it.

MARRIAGE AND CHILDREN

If the Bible mandate for man and woman is to bear children, then it follows that the business of marriage must be taken seriously. Marriage is not just another alternative on the smorgasbord of lifestyles from which our society is free to choose. To treat marriage lightly is also to treat the command of God for creation lightly.

Granted, not every person is called to marry. Jesus recognized that there were those who renounced marriage in order to pursue the Kingdom of God (Matt. 19:12). The Apostle Paul expressed his wish that all men could remain single as he himself was in order to devote more time and energy to serving the Lord. But in the same breath he also realized that such a calling is a gift from God. What is evident in all of this is that whether one follows the customary course in marriage or whether one is called specifically by God to a time of singleness, both are used to expand the Kingdom of God in their own way.

It is marriage, however, that is God's plan for man in being fruitful and filling the earth. It is marriage that paves the way to the future and brings stability to society. I say marriage because it is the only prescribed arrangement that can successfully appoint itself to produce and nurture children without them becoming a significant liability to society. Such a statement, of course, immediately brings several questions to mind. Why marriage? Does marriage obligate its partners to produce children? And do children produced outside the marital relationship constitute a liability to society?

If one were to ask modern man to explain the basis for marriage, he might be hard pressed for an answer. Indeed, many Christians might be equally pressed. Not that we have any shortage of books, films, and tapes on marriage. Peruse any of the innumerable books on marriage and you will discover plenty of titles that describe what marriage is—it is caring, companionship, commitment, covenant, etc. There are even more titles that will tell you how to have a good marriage, a better marriage, or a fantastic marriage! Many people simply assume marriage exists because God ordained that it should be. But why did God ordain it?

Marriage exists *primarily* for one reason—to produce children. From a creation point of view, it is the only way man is able to meet the responsibility of his divinely ordered task, which is to subdue and rule over the earth. Man alone is created to be God's vice-regent on earth with the responsibility to govern the created order.

Such a responsibility, however, necessitates two conditions. The first is that man be given the authority to fulfill this divine function of ruling; and, second, that he be given the capability to do so.

The authority to rule comes by virtue of the fact that man is created to be the image of God on earth and is commissioned by God to be a representative of His being. The psalmist David recognized this commission in Psalm 8 where he wrote:

What is man that you are mindful of him, the son of man that you care for him? You made him a little lower than the heavenly beings and crowned him with glory and honor. You made him ruler over the works of your hands; you put everything under his feet. . . . (vv. 4-6)

Commenting on this passage Artur Weiser observes:

> The King of the universe has even gone so far as to install man as the King of the earth and to "crown" him with the regalia of "majesty and glory" which really are the attributes of God's own appearance. It is in this sense that we can speak here of man being created "in the image of God and after his likeness."[4]

The capability of fulfilling this task of ruling creation comes by virtue of the fact that man is created in the image of God as male and female. The man by himself is incapable of being fruitful, but with the woman, who is created to be his helper, there is a complementarity which enables them to be fruitful and thereby take dominion of the earth. It is this complementarity, found in human sexual differentiation, that becomes the foundation of marriage, for it is the only way of bearing physical fruit for God.

Most anthropologists are agreed that the natural movement in marriage is toward children. The very essence of marriage, Bronislaw Malinowski observed, is "parenthood and above all maternity."[5] Even if one argues that love is the primary reason for marriage, we very quickly see that love being converted into a biological expression which consummates the marriage. Hence, marriage is defined in terms of becoming "one flesh" (cf. Gen. 2:24; Matt 19:3-12). Moreover, whenever male and female join together in the complementarity of one flesh, the potential for new life exists. It does not take a degree in biology to understand that if one follows the standard recipe of sexual intercourse, all the ingredients are present to create life.

One may wonder, too, why the sex drive is such a powerful, dominant force among humans. It is nearly as powerful as the basic drives of survival to eat or to seek shelter and safety. Perhaps common to all of man's strongest drives, including sex, is that they constrain man to preserve life. Can it just be coincidence that one of man's strongest drives is connected to the fruitfulness of life? Or could it be part of God's design to insure that man would indeed follow His plan in bearing children?

With the potential of life so closely associated with sexual intercourse, it is important that an environment be created in which that life can be nurtured and grown. Thus, along with the responsibility of procreation comes the responsibility to nurture and care for the children which result from it. Such responsibility depends upon the mutual sacrifice of the man and the woman in a permanent commitment to one another (Gen. 2:24; Matt 19:4-6).

But does marriage *obligate* its partners to produce children? And what about those couples who *cannot* produce children? If we were still living in the kind of world which existed when God gave man his commission to be fruitful and rule over the created order, the answer would be an unqualified *yes*—our obligation in marriage is to produce children. Indeed, there are those who feel this obligation still holds true and that God should be the one to determine how many children we should have.[6]

However, we no longer live in Paradise. When man disobeyed God in the Garden (Gen. 3), he handed his authority over to Satan and lost his right to rule (Luke 4:6; 1 John 5:19). Through the Fall man's capacity to be fruitful for God was also greatly impaired. Its result brought pain to childbirth, and the capability of every married couple producing children was sabotaged.

Because of the Fall, not every couple *can* produce children. But what about those who can and won't, or those who can but choose to limit the number of children they have to one or two? Do we have the right to choose whether or not we have children or to limit the number of children we want? This seems to me a difficult question to answer, but one deserving careful thought.

Again, sin has so affected the human personality that even though we might have the biological capability of being fruitful, we do not always possess the mental or spiritual faculties to properly nurture children once we have them. Sadly, some children will not be properly loved and nurtured. The answer here, as in all things, is to surrender one's life and personality to the Lordship of Jesus Christ. Still, even as Christians, there are areas of personal struggle (for example, violent anger) which may work against nurturing our children. These areas of failure must be dealt with according to the power of Christ.

This is not to say that not having children or limiting the

number of children one has is God's plan for one's life. Indeed, it may even be subversive to it. Though there are realities which must be responsibly considered before having children, strong warnings can be issued to those who deliberately choose to forego having children.

The first warning goes to those couples who view raising children as a hindrance to their own personal pleasure and fulfillment. Selfishness has serious consequences. The desire for self-gratification and materialism can be a trap set by the Enemy to lead people away from God.

The second warning is for those who insist that they have the right to choose for themselves whether they want to have children or not. As psychologist James Dobson points out:

> . . . there's something ambiguous about insisting on a "right" which would mean the end of the human race if universally applied! If women wearied of childbearing for a mere thirty-five years on earth, the last generation of mortals would grow old and die, leaving no offspring to reproduce.[7]

I would maintain that while sexual intercourse in marriage may serve to bring intimacy and the expression of love, its primary purpose is to produce children or at least to remind husband and wife of their potential to bear fruit for God.

It is interesting that when God promised Abraham that He would multiply his descendants as the stars of heaven, He sealed the covenant with the requirement that all of Abraham's descendants be circumcised (Gen. 17). Thus, every time an Israelite had sex he was reminded of his part in the covenant—namely, to multiply and so fulfill the purpose of God.

One last question remains—is marriage necessary to the bearing and raising of children? Apart from marriage, are they a liability to society?

That question leads us to another question: who carries the responsibility for children born outside of marriage?

In our society, the answer is evident: women do! (Morally, it is obvious that both the man and woman—father and mother—should assume responsibility. But on average it is left up to the mother.) Apart from impregnation, it is the woman who carries the responsibility of the new life. Her tie to the child is inescapable by virtue of her sexuality. It is in *her* body that life is created. It is in *her* womb that life is developed. It is through *her* breasts that life is nourished.

Biologically, after the man impregnates the woman, he does not by necessity have to be there during the pregnancy or at birth. The woman is the bearer of children, and it is with the woman that the children often stay. According to the National Census Bureau, 23 percent of American children live with only one parent, and 90 percent of all these single-parent children under the age of eighteen live with their mothers.[8] While many of these women are single parents as a result of divorce, the number of never-married mothers is growing. Over 5 percent of our nation's 62.5 million children live with mothers who were never married; that translates into more than three million children. Seventy-four percent of these mothers will depend on public assistance.[9]

Not only will society pay a price in raising these children and supporting their mothers, but also in reforming many of them. Single women were not meant to be the primary role models for adolescent boys; and although women are not totally to blame for this, they often fail in their heroic attempt to raise their sons rightly. Over half a million children were admitted to our nation's juvenile detention and correctional facilities in 1984; of these 86 percent were male and 61 percent were white.[10] Further research into our nation's prisons reveals that the overwhelming majority of inmates had no male role model while growing up.

We must recognize that the ability to successfully raise and nurture children is directly related to the success of a marriage, and the success of marriage is built on sex roles.

SEX ROLES IN MARRIAGE

When God created man as male and female and commanded them to be fruitful and multiply, He established a social order, the foundation of which is marriage. More often than not, it is love, mysteriously ignited by a mutual encounter of body and soul, which persuades men and women that they ought to be together. But it is marriage which brings the complementarity of men and women into line with the created order. And it is marriage which further orchestrates the distinctions of the sexes into a harmonious social order.

While men and women are both human beings, they are not identical beings. They have each received a different stamp which calls them to experience life differently from the other. As George Carey has pointed out:

Man's experience of life as a man, and a woman's experience as a woman, necessarily means that the one is excluded from a range of human experience which belongs to the other.[11]

Thus, a woman's role and function in society will usually be defined by that which she experiences as a woman. We should not be surprised, nor should we be embarrassed that most women will find their greatest sense of satisfaction and fulfillment in the roles of wife and mother. No one need remind a woman of this; it is, after all, what she has been reminded of all her life. Her monthly cycle reminds her of her ever-present potential to bear new life, the development of her breasts reminds her of her ability to nurture that life, and her maternal desire for babies, even at a young age, all connect her to the roles of marriage and motherhood.

A man, on the other hand, has no such reminders. His role does not unfold naturally, and there are no long-term rhythms in his sexuality that tell him what his function in society is. His one-act sexual repertoire can be repeated continually without biologically requiring him to accept the consequences. This does not mean that he is left without a role or function in society, but only that he must discover what it is in a different way. A man discovers his role through marriage.

In marriage we see how the distinctions of the sexes work in harmony to accomplish the purpose of God. The woman's sexuality necessarily connects her to children and the domestic scene. She cannot disconnect herself from nine months of pregnancy (although new technology in surrogate parenting threatens this more each day) and the lactation and nursing which by nature belong to the woman. It is not by accident that her maternal nature is given to caring and nurturing.

By contrast, the man's sexuality connects him only briefly with producing children. He performs his act and biologically he is done. While he loves his children and provides the important role model of male sexuality (especially important to his sons), he is not, nor can he be the nurturer a woman is. But this is advantageous to the family. His desire for progeny which connects him to the future must come through his love for one woman and his commitment to provide for their well-being. He can no longer philander as a single man, for the woman's need for security and protection will not allow it. His responsibility to provide, evoked by love, gives him the long-range commitment necessary to connect him with his family.

Suddenly we see the perfection of the divine plan. The design is so evident that one would have to ignore the obvious differences and complementarity of the sexes to suggest that male and female roles should be otherwise. Marriage is God's plan for producing, nurturing, and providing for children. Marriage and family expert James Dobson affirms that:

> When a society is composed of millions of individual families that are established on this plan, then the nation will be strong and stable. It is the great contribution marriage makes to civilization. But in its absence, ruination is inevitable. When men have no reason to harness their energies in support of home, then drug abuse, alcoholism, sexual intrigue, job instability, and aggressive behavior can be expected to run unchecked throughout culture, and that is the beginning of the end.[12]

Moreover, women pose a similar threat to society when they abandon the role of wife and mother. As wife, her long-term stability bridles the potentially destructive aggressions of the male. As George Gilder observes, single men constitute the greatest threat to our society. He notes:

> Men commit over 90 percent of major crimes of violence, 100 percent of the rapes, 95 percent of the burglaries. They comprise 94 percent of our drunken drivers, 70 percent of suicides, 91 percent of offenders against family and children. More specifically, the chief perpetrators are single men. Single men comprise between 80 and 90 percent of most of the categories of social pathology, and on the average they make less money than any other group in society—yes, less than single women or working women. As any insurance actuary will tell you,

single men are also less responsible about their bills, their driving, and other personal conduct. Together with the disintegration of the family, they contribute our leading social problem.[13]

Marriage, however, channels this male aggression to the benefit of the family and society. Indeed, if a man is to win the love of a woman he must show her he will be responsible or she will not have him. Thus, it is to *her* rhythm of life that marriage and society must conform if either is to survive.

As mother the woman is the vessel in which the ultimate values of a culture reside. Because of her close connectedness to her children, she will bear the strongest influence on their values and morals. Society is largely what women determine it should be, which means her "career" as a mother is the most powerful and influential responsibility in society. If she forfeits her role to the day-care center in pursuit of any other career, she asks more from society than it is able to give.

Despite the forces in our society which wage war against the traditional roles of men and women and call for the abandonment of all sexual distinctions, we must affirm the distinctions of the sexes and the roles they play in preserving the stability of family and society. To abandon those distinctions is not only to abandon the future, but to abandon the image of God in man as well. Finally, if we fail to recognize the importance of maintaining our sexual differentiation, we will open the door to every sexual perversion one can imagine. Such a departure will surely lead us down the road to destruction.

THREE

THE ROAD
TO DESTRUCTION

*D*espite the arguments of psychologists, sociologists, and sexo-logists to the contrary, sexual perversion is a fact of modern society. But, of course, we'll have none of that talk. It sounds so narrow-minded, so bigoted, so out of step with the times. After all, who in our sexually "sophisticated" society can really define what is perverse and what is not?

The Supreme Court can't. Its own definition of what consti-tutes sexually obscene (perverse) material is so broad that it can be interpreted to exclude almost anything from being considered ob-scene or perverse.[1] And the church hasn't. Many of its various denominations continue to debate the ordination of homosexuals. And social scientists won't. As one sociologist put it, "I don't believe in the existence of human absolutes . . . sexuality is simply one more facet of humanity that changes along with the rest, as culture changes and beliefs change."[2]

So society tells us to be tolerant, to mind our own business. What may be perverse to one might mean sexual liberation to another. What may be seen as a life of perversion to me might simply be considered an alternative lifestyle to you. What two consenting adults decide to do is their business, as long as it doesn't hurt anyone. Perversion is in the eye of the beholder!

Indeed, this trend toward greater tolerance by society can be seen in our changing sexual vernacular. Noting these changes Dr. John Gagnon, professor of sociology at the State University of New York, Stony Brook states:

Words such as nice and virtue, grace and sinfulness, gave way to such terms as normal and abnormal, mature and perverse. Today we hear with equal frequency expressions such as "meaningful relationships" and "sexual variations" (instead of "deviations").[3]

Society has redefined its terms in order to make acceptable acts which have always been regarded as unacceptable. Who wants to participate in something as awful as "sexual perversion" when he can participate in a "meaningful relationship" and be doing the same thing? Gagnon goes on to say:

Struggles over the meaning of words are not merely semantic jousts. Words are symbols that influence action, and what we feel toward persons and acts depends on whether we define them to be perverse or positive. What we call things is both a source of meaning and a justification for behavior.[4]

I am afraid that if Gagnon is right and we allow society to redefine sexual perversion in the name of "sexual variations" or "alternative lifestyle" or "mutual consent" or anything else, we are in danger of losing three important truths. First, we will lose the truth that sexual perversion does exist. Alternative lifestyles are those which break away from the natural order and hence constitute a perversion of that order. We are not given countless sexual options from which to choose. We are given one according to the natural order in which God created us as male and female. To follow any other pattern or alternative is to distort or pervert God's design for human sexuality.

The second truth we are in danger of losing is that sexual perversion has consequences in the life of the individual or society which deviates from the natural order. There is an axiom which states that you can choose to sin, but you cannot choose the consequences. You cannot distort the use of something and expect to get undistorted results. God intended for us to use our sexuality for the purpose for which it was created; any use of our sexuality which deviates from its purpose will bring severe consequences. The remaining chapters of this book focus on this truth.

And third, if we deny that sexual perversion exists by redefining it so that it sounds more acceptable to us, we are in danger of losing the truth that something can and should be done about it. There is hope and help for those who are caught in sexual perversions, but they must see their perversion for what it is before they can move back into God's intended purpose for their sexuality. As long as we see sexual perversion as an option which we are free to choose, rather than a sin against the created order, we will never accept the help we need. We must first understand what sexual perversion is.

Sexual perversion is the denial of or deviation from the proper and natural function for which the sexes were created. The Bible defines sexual perversion in Romans 1 as exchanging "natural relations for unnatural ones." Implied in this definition of perversion is that there is a normal or natural function of human sexuality which can be deviated from or somehow distorted.

The natural order is based on the distinction of the sexes and is understood in terms of their complementarity. In the natural order men and women are called together through an attraction to the opposite sex. The anatomical distinctions in the male and female genitalia are designed as perfect complements. The structure of the human body allows us to participate in the greatest act of human creation while encountering one another as persons face to face. The natural order is that this dynamic encounter between male and female be fruitful or at least potentially fruitful.

Therefore, sexual variations that deviate from the complementarity of our anatomy or reject the potential for the fruitfulness for which sex was designed may be considered deviations of the natural order and thus perverted. Thus acts of homosexuality, bestiality, and oral-anal sex are practices which fall into the unnatural order and are considered perversions. Moreover, sexual experiences which prohibit the meeting of persons, such as voyeurism or fantasizing and masturbating over pornographic material, also constitutes a kind of perversion.

If sexual perversion is a departure from the created order, then by implication it must be considered as rebellion against God. It is God who established the natural order; and to reject it, by destroying or perverting it, is to reject the One who created it. Sexual perversion, then, is sin because it is rebellion against God and as such will lead men to destruction (Rom. 6:23). But what leads a person down the road to destruction? Why would anyone distort something if it was the best to start with?

People are not born as sexual perverts. Nor do many people intentionally purpose to become one. While I have had many occasions to counsel and pray with people caught in sexually deviant lifestyles, I have yet to have someone come into my office and say, "I can't understand it. One day I just woke up addicted to pornography," or, "One day I woke up and I was a compulsive voyeur," or, "One day I woke up and I was a practicing homosexual."

Instead, what I usually hear are comments like, "I just got caught in a habit I couldn't stop. I never meant for it to go this far—I just sort of drifted into it." In other words, most people do not normally jump from normal sexuality to sexual perversion in one full motion. Rather, the movement away from normal sexuality to perversion is usually a progression of choices, circumstances, and events.

A number of factors appear to work together to lead persons into sexual perversion. These include personality traits, a domineering mother or the rejection of a father, the choice one makes to feed sexual fantasies, or even a traumatic sexual encounter as a child. But what is often ignored is the larger context within which the individual exists and which creates an environment for the particular factors just mentioned to take root and have influence in a person's life. The particular ethos or spirit of a culture affects what a person does as much as anything. If the cultural ethos is one of moral depravity, as ours presently is, then many will be led astray who normally would not be.

I believe there is an ethos of the world which gathers strength from the spiritual condition of a culture and in turn can influence it towards an even greater depravity. It is like a hurricane which gathers strength as it blows, and the more it blows the stronger it becomes. In the same way, when people within a culture share a certain point of view, it gathers enough momentum to alter the opinions of others who in turn lend strength to the idea until it becomes the prevailing point of view. The new point of view then paves the way for more radical views to be built upon it. I suppose it is somewhat akin to the Hegelian dialectic.

Thus, for example, when homosexuals began coming out of

their closets in the midsixties the winds of sexual "liberation" were already blowing. With the pill in their possession, and a cynical attitude towards what was considered a hypocritical Judeo-Christian ethic, America's attitude toward sex was changing. There was a permissive, "if it feels good do it" spirit in the air. And as the wind kept blowing, it blew open a few closet doors.

Although persecuted at first, homosexuals were being carried on the wind of a sexual revolution. By 1975 both the American Psychiatric Association and the Psychological Association of America had classified homosexuality as normal behavior. With perhaps the strongest lobbying effort in America, and the support of newsmen, filmmakers, and television producers, the homosexual subculture has quickly moved to the forefront of American society.

The result has been the enfranchisement of homosexuality as a valid lifestyle. Despite the fact that homosexuality flouts God's law, perverts and corrupts public morality, undermines the family, and presents a monumental health hazard to society, no one is allowed to speak out against it without being branded a homophobe. This is the spirit of the world we must resist. We must not compromise our understanding of human sexuality because of the pressure put on us by society. Certainly we must show compassion and be moved to offer help and encouragement, but that is something different from compromising. We must hold fast to the Word of God. For when society rejects God's Word as it speaks to the created order, it will, as in the case of the individual, follow a progression that moves from the natural order to a place of moral decadence.

That this is true is made clear in the first chapter of Romans.

ROMANS 1:18-32

In Romans 1 we have a picture of what happens when man deliberately rejects the truth about God as it is revealed in the created order, and we are shown the road that leads to destruction.

The Case Against Man (Rom. 1:10-20)

Beginning in verses 18-20, God's case against man is set forth:

> The wrath of God is being revealed from heaven against all the godlessness and wickedness of men who suppress the truth by their wickedness, since what may be known about God is plain to them, because God has made it plain to them. For since the

creation of the world God's invisible qualities—his eternal power and divine nature—have been clearly seen, being understood from what has been made, so that men are without excuse.

Two things are evident from this passage of Scripture. First, the truth of God and His purpose is made known in the created order. Through observing and understanding creation man can postulate the existence of God. But it is also through the created order that God's purpose for man is revealed. While this observation has far-reaching implications, it at least includes the fact that the morphology of man's anatomy (since it is part of the observable created order) gives him a clue as to how it ought to be used. And indeed, as we saw in Chapter 1, it is useful for understanding the nature of God.

The purpose of God in the created order is made plain. Male and female understand that they are differentiated from one another, but also discover that the differentiation is in fact a complementarity. They know what to do, and when they do it they are fruitful. This fellowship reveals a design and order which leads man to deduce a Designer and brings a consciousness of God.

The second thing we learn is that man has willfully suppressed the truth about God's nature as it is revealed in the created order. Moreover, his choice to disregard the clear evidence from creation concerning God's nature has left him "without excuse." This suppression or willful disregard for the truth is the first step on the road to destruction. This holds true for a nation as well as for an individual.

But man cannot live in a complete moral vacuum. If he disregards the truth, he must replace it with something. So he exchanges the truth of God for a lie.

The Great Exchange (vv 21-24)

Although man had a knowledge of God, he refused to acknowledge Him as God. Man thus severed himself from the ability to know and practice truth and set himself up in the worst kind of idolatry—humanism, the worship of himself.

For although they knew God, they neither glorified him as God nor gave thanks to him, but their thinking became futile and their foolish hearts were darkened. Although they claimed to be wise, they became fools and exchanged the glory of the immortal God for images made to look like mortal man and birds and animals and reptiles. (vv. 21-23)

When man rejects God, his mind is given to futile thinking. He has no source of moral truth and certainly no moral absolutes. Dostoyevski was right when he said, "If God does not exist, everything is permitted." The essence of humanism is that man lives in a godless universe where nothing exists above the natural order, and man is thus left to define his own meaning and purpose to life.

The blasphemy in all of this is found in verse 23 where the very things that God created out of nothing are now placed above Him. Ultimately, the rejection of God and man's exaltation of himself leaves him purposeless in life. He does not know where he comes from, who he is, or where he is going. Because he is now left to define his own existence, all that matters is what he himself determines should matter. Stripped of absolutes and authentic boundaries, he is able to pursue his lusts as far as they will take him. What he fails to see, however, is that his lusts will progressively take him further down the road to destruction.

The Road to Destruction

Once man has suppressed the truth and rejected God, the process of destruction takes place in three steps. In verses 24, 26, and 28 of Romans 1 we find God progressively giving man over to greater moral corruption and sexual excess.

The first step is found in verses 24 and 25, and it is characterized by excessive sexual desire and practice.

Therefore God gave them over in the sinful desires of their hearts to sexual impurity for the degrading of their bodies with one another. They exchanged the truth of God for a lie, and worshiped and served created things rather than the Creator—who is forever praised.

As we read this passage, we must be careful not to assume that God has in any way initiated man's moral spiral downward. That God "gave them over" is not the initiation of God, but the consequence of man's deliberate decision to suppress the truth of God and replace it with a lie. Once man rejected God, God chose not to prevent man from falling into the consequences of his rebellion. Man is thus abandoned to the "sinful desires" of his heart.

The French philosopher Blaise Pascal once said that every man has a God-shaped vacuum in his heart. If man rejects God, he will most certainly fill that vacuum with something else. This is idolatry—replacing our need for God with something else, exchanging the worship of God with a lust after creation. Man thus replaces God with the lusts of his creaturely existence.

Perhaps the strongest lust man has is his sexual lust. However, sexual lust is insufficient to fill the God-shaped vacuum of man's heart. Sexual lust is insatiable when it is used to fill the desire of our heart. That is the nature of lust—it continually feeds off itself and must be constantly replenished. This is what we see happening in the Biblical passage—man pursuing the natural function of sex in extreme excess. Moreover, since any Biblical restraints man might have otherwise had have been removed, the sinful desires or lusts of his heart are given to further degradation. His sexual lusts carry him further in his perversion and further down the road to destruction.

The second stage is characterized by God giving man over to indulgence in unnatural sexual functions (vv. 26, 27).

> Because of this, God gave them over to shameful lusts. Even their women exchanged natural relations for unnatural ones. In the same way the men also abandoned natural relations with women and were inflamed with lust for one another. Men committed indecent acts with other men, and received in themselves the due penalty for their perversion.

The suppression of the truth of God, which starts in the mind (v. 18), now expresses itself through a gross distortion of the natural order. Man exchanges the natural function of heterosexual sex for an unnatural or perverted expression—namely, homosexuality. Paul expresses the vileness of this perversion by first noting that even the women have abandoned their natural function by having unnatural (lesbian) relations with one another.

We should not suppose that Paul's listing the women first in this passage expresses anything of the notion that women are more inclined to fall into homosexual relations than men and thereby pave the way for men to follow. This has not historically been the case. Rather, listing the women first accentuates the grossness of the evil.[5]

However, another interesting point of view has been put forth concerning this passage. Mary Pride suggests that verse 26 does not refer to lesbianism at all. She observes that the text only says that the females exchanged their natural function for that which is against nature. Pride connects the woman's natural function to the etymology of the word *woman*, or more accurately female, which comes from a root word meaning "to nurse or give suck." Thus the natural function of the female is to bear and nurture children. On account of this association, she proposes that

> . . . when women exchange their natural function of childbearing and motherliness for that which is "against nature" (that is, trying to behave sexually like a man), the men tend to abandon the natural sexual use of the women and turn to homosexuality. When men stop seeing women as mothers, sex loses its sacredness. Sex becomes "recreational," and therefore the drive begins to find new kicks.[6]

In either case, the point being made is that the natural order is abandoned for that which is against nature. Again, we see that when man rejects God he also rejects God's purpose for the created order, so that male and female distinctions are no longer important. When man abandons the natural use of the woman in favor of homosexual relations, he cannot perform sexually without distorting the created order. Men have no complementarity with each other, and therefore they must do what is unnatural by performing oral and anal acts of perversion against one another. Sex in this context has no purpose except to serve the insatiable lusts of man's darkened heart.

Furthermore, as man's heart is hardened, he begins to see his perverted condition as normal. As we have already noted above, homosexual behavior is now considered normal by the Psychological Association of America, while most of the general population takes at least a passive attitude toward it. America should take warning. Throughout history one of the indications that a society was in decline was an increased acceptance of and participation in homosexual behavior.

Such perversion in society could not take place unless the human mind was so darkened that it could no longer discern the difference between right and wrong—which is exactly what happens on the road to destruction.

The third step is characterized by a depraved mind (vv. 28-32).

> Furthermore, since they did not think it worthwhile to retain the knowledge of God, he gave them over to a depraved mind, to do what ought not to be done. . . . Although they know God's righteous decree that those who do such things deserve death, they not only continue to do these very things but also approve of those who practice them.

The longest list of sins in the New Testament is found between verses 28 and 32. They are all the result of God giving man over to a depraved mind. The depraved mind is literally the "worthless" or "unreliable" mind. It is worthless because it no longer has the ability to discriminate right from wrong. Hence it has no standards of behavior.

Although all men have a conscience which bears witness to the moral quality of their behavior, the conscience of the depraved mind has been so corrupted that it is no longer sensitive to the truth of God (cf. 1 Tim. 4:2; Titus 1:15). Man is therefore able to participate in perverted activities and encourage others to do so also (v. 32).

The third stage is by far the most dangerous. With no moral absolutes to govern human behavior, permission is given for every man to do what is right in his own eyes. This is the very condition that precipitated the judgment of God on man in the days of Noah when the Lord saw that "every inclination of the thoughts of his heart was only evil all the time" (Gen. 6:5).

The mind of modern man has reached this stage, and slowly but surely the actions which spring forth from it are bringing Western society closer and closer to destruction. The stage is set and the play has begun. Man has already pinned his rejection of the natural order to the philosophical presupposition that there is no God. He has suppressed the truth of God and replaced it with a lie.

THE ROAD TO DESTRUCTION

The lie is that there is no Sovereign Holy God who owns and rules creation. Instead, man himself is the creator of his destiny; he alone will determine his moral value system. But his depraved mind cannot portend the actions that will result from the lie.

Man cannot see that when babies are destroyed before they are born because they are seen as unwanted intrusions or social liabilities, the stage is set for the destruction of the elderly, the mentally or physically handicapped, or anyone else deemed a liability. He cannot see that when sex is taken from its intended purpose, sexual distinctions become unimportant and the stage is set for every possible sexual perversion one can imagine. Nor does he see that the acts which follow such perversion will undermine marriage, the family, and ultimately the very society they hold together.

Man cannot see the forces in the world about him that cause him to deny the distinctions between the sexes and which will eventually bring him down the road to destruction.

In the remainder of this book we shall seek to expose those forces in society which deny the distinction of the sexes or pervert God's intended purpose for our sexuality and which lead men to rebel against the purpose of God for creation. For if we refuse to acknowledge those distinctions, we will surely follow the road to destruction.

PART II

DISMANTLING THE SEXES

FEMINISM

*G*od has a purpose for the sexes. So do the feminists. And the two are not the same.

The former sees the distinction of the sexes as necessary to bear the image of God in man and to accomplish God's purpose on earth, and it must therefore be preserved. The latter sees the distinction of the sexes as an obstacle to women's rights and personal freedom, and it must therefore be obliterated. Perhaps nothing hastens the destruction of the sexes as much as the feminist movement.

While feminism is no longer personified in the plain, braless woman of the sixties and seventies wearing jeans and T-shirts, sneakers and steel-rimmed glasses, its ideology has remained the same.[1] And although their visibility may not be as prominent as it was in the seventies, a significant number of women consider themselves feminists. In an article entitled "The Myth of Post Feminism," the June 1986 issue of *MS* magazine reported a Gallup poll which found that a majority of women surveyed (56 percent) identified themselves as feminists.[2] Despite the failure of passage for the Equal Rights Amendment, feminist philosophy has managed to insinuate itself within our nation's schools and colleges by means of unrelenting propaganda by the intellectual elite. As we shall see, feminism is a conscious ideology which deliberately seeks to dismantle the Biblical understanding of sexual differentiation and complementarity. As a result, radical feminists have attacked everything that supports traditional roles of men and women including God, the Bible, marriage, heterosexuality, the family, and children.

Ex-feminist Mary Pride warns us that even

Christians have accepted feminists' "moderate" demands for family planning and careers while rejecting the "radical" side of feminism—meaning lesbianism and abortion. What most do not see is that one demand leads to the other. *Feminism is a totally self-consistent system aimed at rejecting God's role for women.* Those who adopt any part of its lifestyle can't help picking up its philosophy.[3]

The basic tenet of feminist philosophy is that women constitute an oppressed class treated as inferiors on the basis of their sex. One liberationist writes:

Women are enslaved: the enslavement and indirect murder of women [come] by means of legislation and moral (i.e., immoral) dictates against abortion, birth control, and lesbianism.[4]

The oppressors, of course, are men who subjugate women through patriarchal religion and economic dominance, both of which deny women their equal status with men and their inherent worth as human beings. Christianity is especially seen as a bulwark of misogyny because through centuries of teachings on marriage and the subordination of wives to their husbands it has relegated women to such "meaningless" labors as childbearing, the nurturing of children, and homemaking. Thus one feminist, who herself claims to be a Christian, writes: "We need not minimize the radicality of women's oppression in varied cultures and communities nor minimize Christianity's continuing involvement in that oppression, but we must not let that recognition confirm us in a posture of victimization."[5]

And how is the victimization of women stopped and equality asserted? Women's liberationists are unanimous: it is by denying all sex roles based on male and female distinctions. Thus, Betty Freidan suggests that if women are to realize their inherent worth as human beings, they must refuse to identify themselves with their image of housewives and mothers and pursue careers outside the home.[6] In Shulamith Firestone's book *The Dialectic of Sex* we find a more radical attempt to blur sexual distinctions. Firestone asserts that the *biological* reproductive functions of the sexes are responsible for creating a class system which inherently leads to an unequal distribution of power. The natural reproductive differences of the sexes leave women bound to the tyranny of the childbearing and child-rearing role of society. The biological family creates an imbalance which leads directly to the first division into economic classes.[7]

But Firestone is persistent. She does not abandon the case for women's liberation even though she admits that sexual inequality is based in biology. Instead, she focuses her attack on the biological family. The underclass (women) must revolt and seize control of the means of reproduction, by which she means the new technology for artificial reproduction in test tubes, as well as the social institutions of childbearing and child-rearing.

> . . . the end goal of feminist revolution must be, unlike that of
> the first feminist movement, not just the elimination of male
> *privilege* but of the sex *distinction* itself: genital differences
> between human beings would no longer matter culturally.[8]

There would be pan-sexuality and androgynous people—that is, no men and women. Reproduction would be through artificial means, child-care in group form—which would apparently end the subordination of children to adults. With the abolition of the family would go the psychology of power in which economic classes are grounded.

Thus, for Firestone the feminist revolution would be an ultimate one. It involves: (1) the liberation of women from the tyranny of reproductive biology by every means available, and the diffusion of the childbearing and child-rearing role to society as a whole; (2) the full self-determination of women and children. This requires their economic independence. A feminist socialism, according to Firestone, also involves an equal distribution of wealth to children; (3) the total integration of women and children into all aspects of society; (4) the freedom of women and children to do whatever they wish sexually.[9]

Kate Millett, in her book *Sexual Politics*, affirms that a feminist revolution would *require* "an end of all traditional sexual inhibitions and taboos, particularly those that most threaten patriarchal monogamous marriage: homosexuality, 'illegitimacy,' adolescent, pre- and extramarital."[10] In other words there would be unrestricted sexual activity of all kinds. In the overthrow of patriarchy and the abolition of sex roles, monogamous marriage and the traditional family would collapse and with it would go the oppression of male supremacy.

In a further effort to "undermine family structure while contributing to the freedom of women," Millett proposes professional collective care of the young. The public care and education of children is an absolutely basic condition for female liberation. As long as every woman is obliged by her anatomy to be the primary caretaker of children, she is prevented from being truly free.[11] The repercussions of such feminist philosophy are nothing less than frightening.

We can see in the feminist quest for liberation that there is more at stake than "equal rights." The ideology of the feminist movement runs much deeper than politics and economics; it cuts to the very core of our Biblical understanding of God and the creation of man in the image of God as male and female. As one set of demands leads to another, the feminists' denial of sexual distinctions between man and woman and their call for the obliteration of all sex roles necessarily requires one to alter the Biblical concepts of marriage, family, and God. Indeed, the feminist position ultimately requires one to ignore or alter the plain teachings of Scripture altogether. Feminism finally sets itself up as its own religion, with woman being worshiped as her own goddess. As we are about to see, it is a thoroughly self-consistent philosophy which sets itself on a course of social and spiritual destruction.

Let's see what the feminists really propose. As much as possible, I will let them tell you in their own words.

WHAT FEMINISM REALLY SAYS

Perhaps nothing stands in the way of the feminist movement as much as Christianity. "Christian ideology has contributed no little to the oppression of women," said the late Simone de Beauvoir.[12] Its teachings on such topics as the creation account of the differentiation and complementarity of the sexes (Gen. 1, 2) and the mutual submission of husbands and wives to one another in love (Eph. 5) are totally antithetical to feminist doctrine.

Judith Dorney, youth ministry director at St. Clement High School and religious educator at both the junior high and high school levels for fourteen years, writes in her essay "Religious Education and the Development of Young Women" that

> . . . submission is sin, for in submission women refuse to accept their full created status as partners with men in the works of God's mission in the world.[13]

So much for serving one another out of love (Gal. 5:13). No matter, since according to feminists any teaching of Christian love militates against sexual equality. Here is what Mary Daly of Harvard Divinity School has to say about Christian love:

> . . . women hooked on churchly love-hysteria are victims of necrophilic love that loves to see women possessed, marching zombie-like in the ranks of the living dead. The strategies of the church love-mongers are essentially the same as those of other pimps, pornographers, woman-batterers, and child molesters. "Love" is intended to hook a woman, making her dependent emotionally and psychologically. She is taught to believe that this "love" is mutual.[14]

Faced with what they consider an oppressive faith, the only solution for Daly and others is to abandon historical Christianity altogether. Such a solution is certainly logical given the tenets of woman's liberation. When one abandons the distinction of the sexes as well as the roles that are built on those distinctions, one must also abandon every system of belief which reinforces those distinctions. Again, Daly is brazen and forthright:

> To put it rather bluntly, I propose that Christianity itself should be castrated by cutting away the products of super male arrogance: the myths of sin and salvation that are simply two diverse symptoms of the same disease. . . . I am suggesting that the idea of salvation uniquely by a male savior perpetuates the problem of patriarchal oppression. . . . Jesus Was A Feminist, But So What? In an admirable and scholarly article Leonard Swidler marshals historical evidence to show convincingly that Jesus was a feminist. What I think I perceive happening in the

rising woman consciousness is an affirmation that goes something like this: "Fine. Wonderful. But even if he wasn't, *I am*."

What is happening now is that these primordial eunuchs [she means women] are rising up to castrate the system that castrates—the great "God-Father" of us all.[15]

Of course, when women's liberation rejects historical Christianity it must also reject some of its most fundamental doctrines; but the rejection ("castration") of God is utterly blasphemous. Nevertheless, Daly is not alone or unique in her position. Naomi Goldenberg arrogantly asserts:

Every woman working to improve her own position in society or that of women in general is bringing about the end of God.

God is going to change. . . . We women are going to bring an end to God. As we take positions in government, in medicine, in law, in business, in the arts and, finally, *in religion,* we will be the end of Him. We will change the world so much that He won't fit anymore.[16] (emphasis mine)

For the radical feminist (that is, a feminist who has simply followed liberationist ideology to its logical conclusion) God is totally incapable of revealing Himself to man, for if He could do so He certainly would have used some other means besides patriarchy. But the fact that what we know about God and His purpose for the sexes comes to us through a patriarchal religion (Judaism) and that He incarnates Himself as a male (Jesus) only suggests to the feminist that the God revealed in the Bible is nothing more than a male invention designed to keep women in bondage to men.

Again such a position brings with it further consequences, for in rejecting the God of the Bible one must reject the Scriptures themselves. Goldenberg suggests that if women are to achieve liberation, they will have to "leave Christ and the Bible behind them."[17] For the feminist, submission to the Word of God is synonomous with submission to male domination. Beverly Harrison writes that obedience as the central paradigm for the practice of the Christian life is antithetical to morality, because obedience to the Word of God means oppression and social injustice to women. It is an ethic of hierarchy which runs counter to individual experience.[18]

"This kind of Christian ethic," Harrison argues, "is designated in theological ethics as a 'Divine Command Ethic.'"

> It presumes to say that "God commands X" constitutes adequate moral justification for accepting that "I ought to do X."[19]

Harrison, however, rejects such an ethic on the basis that "God talk" is sexist and cultural, and therefore all God's words are no longer true or trustworthy for faith or practice. Thus the idea that we ought to obey the Word of God simply because God says so is no justification for doing so. Feminists believe they must appeal to a "higher" authority than the Word of God. And what is that "higher" authority? It is experience—more specifically, women's experience. Since, according to Elisabeth Fiorenze, all Biblical texts are androcentric, "they must be accompanied by a feminist hermeneutic for hearing and interpreting them."[20] The promotion of "women's experience" as the guiding hermeneutical principle pervades feminist writings. Forget about any literal interpretation of the Bible. Don't bother with any knowledge of historical or literary context. Ignore the *analogy* of faith. And never consult the guidance of the Holy Spirit in interpreting the Bible (1 Cor. 2:14).

Thus Peggy Ann Way rejects Biblical authority in favor of "flexible experience."[21] Letty Russel writes: "Experience is the measure that tests interpretation of the gospels."[22] She goes on to suggest elsewhere that the key elements in Biblical interpretation are: (1) suspicion rather than acceptance of Biblical authority; and (2) authority to choose and to reject Biblical texts.[23]

One of the more prominent theologians in the feminist movement is Rosemary Radford Ruether. In her book *Feminism and Christianity* Denise Carmody, chairperson in the Department of Religion at Wichita State University, describes Ruether as

> An admirable woman who has worked both sides of the feminist-Christian relation . . . Seeing Christianity as a foe of her feminine self, Ruether has vowed to oppose it implacably, so long as it remains mired in sexist sin. *Because she is a fine theologian,* however, she has been able to root this opposition in Christianity's own original soil, turning the cry of the biblical prophets for justice against the unjust Christian establishment.[24] (emphasis mine)

Just how fine a theologian Ruether is seems rather dubious. In her work *Woman-Church* she says:

> Since partiarchal texts have exercised such coercive influence on our lives, although perhaps more so among Protestants who give primary authority to Scripture, it is useful as one Woman-Church ritual to exorcize patriarchal texts and thus to break this oppressive power over their lives.[25]

Instead of using Holy Scripture to judge orthodoxy it is, in the hands of feminists, Scripture itself which is being judged. And whatever the feminist theologian judges as oppressive or coercive is liable for exorcism. How is a Biblical text exorcised, one might ask? Ruether suggests the following liturgy:

Exorcism of Patriarchal Texts
A small table with a bell, candle, and the Bible are assembled in the center of the group. A series of texts with clearly oppressive intentions are read. After each reading, the bell is rung as the reader raises up the book. The community cries out in unison, "Out, demons, out!"
Suggested texts in need of exorcism:

—Leviticus 12:1-5 (uncleanliness of women after childbirth)
—Exodus 19:1, 7-9, 14-15 (shunning of women during giving of the Law at Sinai)
—Judges 19 (rape, torture, dismemberment of the concubine)
—Ephesians 5:21-23 (male headship over women compared to the relation of Christ and the church)
—I Timothy 2:11-15 (women told to keep silence in church and to be saved by bearing children because they are second in creation and first in sin)
—I Peter 2:18-20 (slaves exhorted to accept unjust suffering from their masters as a way of sharing in Christ's crucifixion)

At the end of the exorcism, someone says, "These texts and all oppressive texts have lost their power over our lives. We no longer need to apologize for them or try to interpret them as words of truth, but we cast out their oppressive message as expressions of evil and justifications of evil."[26]

To the feminist, then, the final word is not the Word of the Lord, but the word of woman. Woman becomes the measure of all things, and, as in any idolatrous system, the true God of the Bible is inevitably replaced with other gods. Goldenberg asks:

> What sort of religious forces are beginning in this era of death for the great male gods? Surely new gods will be born. Since "gods" always reflect the styles of behavior we see as possible, as our range of the possible expands so must our pantheon.[27]

Emerging from the pantheon is a revival of the Goddess religion and a rising participation in witchcraft. Moving away from theology (the study of God) and toward what feminists call thealogy (the study of the Goddess), the interest in women and religion is no small one. "All over the country women's studies departments are springing up in Universities dedicated to propagating Feminism as religion."[28] In 1986 The Crossing Press published Anne Carson's book *Feminist Spirituality and the Feminine Divine*, which was nothing more than an annotated bibliography listing and describing 739 titles on feminist thealogy, women, and the Goddess religion.[29] Even in the most conservative feminist writings, the only time God is referred to in a positive way is when His name is changed to "Goddess," "Immanent Mother," "Life Force," "Ground of Being," or "Womb of Being." But as James Edwards points out, when feminists do this

> . . . they are not merely switching labels on a product. They are advocating a shift from a transcendent God to a creation-centered deity. God is no longer our Father in heaven, but a "womb covering the earth."[30]

Indeed feminists have little desire to merely switch labels— their goals are more outrageous. Feminist thealogy appeals to a so-called prehistory when women ruled under the divine Goddess and calls women forth to once again adhere to the Goddess tradition. Although hotly contested, Goddess tradition is summarized by anthropologist Sally Binford like this:

> . . . 4,000 or 6,000 years ago, women were powerful, free, and in control of their lives. Society was organized along matriar-

chal lines, and political decisions were made according to female principles that, as we all know, are sensitive, just, and loving. . . . We worshipped the Goddess in temples of great beauty, and priestesses conducted rites celebrating our sexuality. The world was at peace.

Soon, however, this beautiful life was disrupted by patriarchal males who were bent on negative uses of power and who harbored a predilection for warfare. . . . The Goddess was replaced by a vengeful male god and in order to assure his dominance and assuage his jealousy, all records of matriarchal rule and goddess worship were destroyed. Since this takeover, women have been oppressed. The patriarchs took away our knowledge of contraception and forced us into motherhood; they taught us to be ashamed of our sexuality. . . . If only we can reclaim our past, we can once again be strong and free.[31]

On April 23, 1976 at the first national women's conference on women's spirituality, held in a Unitarian church in Boston, fifteen hundred feminists began to reclaim their past. Naomi Goldenberg recounts what happened:

After listening attentively to two addresses . . . the audience became very active . . . they chanted, "The Goddess Is Alive— Magic Is Afoot." The women evoked the Goddess with dancing, stomping, clapping, and yelling. They stood on pews and danced barebreasted on the pulpit and amid hymn books.

In fact, the women were angry at all religions of the fathers and took this opportunity to mock and defy those religions in a church they had rented for the occasion. . . . Proclaiming that the "Goddess Is Alive" in a traditional church setting is proclaiming that . . . being female is divine. . . .[32]

The feminist idolatry of self-worship is stated again by Goldenberg:

Each woman is encouraged to keep a small altar in her home to be used for meditation and for focusing her will. At the Boston conference, women were advised to use mirrors on their altars to represent the Goddess. That way, they would be continually reminded that they were the Goddess and that they had divine beauty, power, and dignity.[33]

As evil as it seems, feminist ideology doesn't stop here. The rejection of God and evocation of the Goddess can ultimately play into the hands of Satanic influence and occultism. Anne Carson states that because the Goddess is supreme in the feminist tradition, "many feminists consider witchcraft to be a true women's religion."[34] One active feminist who became a witch explains why.

> Witches want to change the internal picture that Jewish and Christian women have of a male god in heaven so that women will no longer accept rule by males on earth.[35]

Certainly not every feminist has or will become a witch, although feminist ideology can certainly take a woman in that direction. But whether one follows the more radical excesses of feminist ideology toward the Goddess religion and witchcraft or not, the final agenda of even the most conservative feminism is the same—denial and destruction of male and female differentiation and complementarity. For the feminist, complementarity can only mean the subordination of woman to man, and subordination always means inferiority, inequality, and male oppression. As one author states:

> Women's liberationists reject the idea of a complementary relationship between the sexes, with each group assigned different but mutually appropriate behavior. Instead, they seek a symmetrical relationship with each sex producing essentially similar behavior.
> . . . (otherwise) the relationship is perceived as one of oppressor and oppressed. . . . Consequently, many traditional female tasks [especially child-rearing] are rejected by women's lib participants. . . .[36]

Beverly Harrison, introduced in the foreword of her book as a woman distinctive in the field of feminist ethics "because of her simultaneous commitments to historical research, social analysis, philosophical integrity, the *Christian community and ministry*," issues a similar challenge to traditional sex roles.

This challenge is important to the feminist ethic because religions' justifications for sex roles remain powerful. One of the most pernicious justifications is teleological natural law, where-in nature . . . is viewed as the mirror of God's intention for human behavior. Two key phrases that indicate the presence of such a natural law theory in relationship to sex roles are "com-plementarity" and "according to the design of the creator," which usually mean that males and females have their respec-tive natures and that from their natures, which are divinely or naturally established, flow certain social roles appropriate to each.[37]

Harrison goes on to state that there is no such thing as male and female natures and that sex role rigidity is destructive to mature interpersonal relations.[38] Feminism thus ignores the central truth that society depends upon sex roles for its survival. Instead it advocates the idea that men and women can interchange their roles without substantially altering society. But what these advocates of liberation do not realize is that once the devil of role differentiation has been swept out, seven new feminist devils come into the empty house, bringing more bondage and oppression than ever before. Commenting on woman's condition described in the feminist writ-ings of Shulamith Firestone, Joan Cassell observes:

> Firestone writes of the *destructive* choice offered women to-day; they can marry, be placed on a pedestal, transformed into a possession or appendage, or become "the other woman" used and misused to prove a man's virility. To escape this *"poisoned love,"* the author outlines several alternatives: a woman can play traditional female games to pay men back; she can join the Search for the Mirage—a nonsexist male; she can have sex without emotion; or she can attempt to form lesbian relation-ships.[39] (emphasis mine)

Some alternatives! Traditional marriage and sex roles are "de-structive" and "poisoned," but casual sex, masturbation, and lesbi-anism are "liberating." Perhaps such conclusions should not sur-prise us. When the truth of God is exchanged for a lie, such deceptions are bound to arise. But then that is the nature of every false religion, including feminism—when one truth is denied, a lie is invented to take its place. Thus when monogamous marriage is denied, promiscuity and homosexuality are affirmed; when childbearing becomes inconvenient, abortion is endorsed; and when the nuclear family is destroyed, state-run child-care will be the result.

This progression is clearly affirmed by the feminists themselves. Let's briefly look at what feminists say about each of these areas.

Men and Marriage

Historian William O'Neill suggests that if women are to secure complete equality, today's feminists will have to challenge the fundamental institutions of monogamy and the nuclear family. "In theory," he states, "women today are free to do as they please; in practice, their heavy obligations as wives and mothers prevent them from exercising the rights they normally enjoy."[40] (Somewhere in all of this you begin to get the feeling that being a husband and a father is pretty easy, where the only obligations are sitting in overstuffed chairs in offices making exciting important decisions in between rounds of golf or fishing or just generally loafing around.)

"In the final analysis," according to O'Neill, "the traditional domestic structure of today's nuclear family is central to women's dilemma in our society. Women's liberation goes to the 'root causes' of the problem and calls for a radical transformation of values, relationships, and institutions."[41] What O'Neill is really saying is that the concept of traditional marriage is a root cause of women's "dilemma" and therefore calls for abandonment. Many women would agree:

. . . the fundamental tragedy of marriage is that it mutilates women; it dooms her to repetition and routine. Marriage as a career for women must be prohibited.[42]

. . . woman must above all be liberated from marriage, which makes her an appendage to man, with the corollary that children are to become the primary responsibility of the state.[43]

. . . women should not enter into marriage; they should be promiscuous and self-sufficient.[44]

. . . it is absurd to pledge oneself for life . . . woman's acceptance of man's right to a commitment on such a day-to-day issue as sexual behavior is tantamount to her acceptance of his total control over her.[45]

But what happens when women abandon marriage in order to pursue feminist ideology? Among other things, sexual activity is removed from God's design and purpose. Women become more like men in their sexual barbarism.

> Sex, yes. Lots of sex, more than ever; one of the advantages of being unattached is that you can sleep around more easily.[46]

> I have lovers because what else is there in life that's so much fun as turning on a new man, interesting him, conquering him?[47]

Or they abandon the need for man entirely for sexual satisfaction.

> . . . once women discover the clitoris rather than the vagina as the source of the orgasm, man becomes sexually expendable and women are able to satisfy themselves or each other.[48]

One thing is certain: while feminists may be willing to give up men and marriage, they are not about to give up on sex. Warning that the media hype of the early eighties about the sexual revolution being over was pure male propoganda, an article carried by *Ms.* magazine stated that "women have come too far to surrender the range of possibilities opened up by a sexual revolution."[49] And what is the range of possibilities opened up by a sexual revolution? Every sexual perversion from promiscuity, to "recreational" masturbation, to lesbianism.

Lesbianism

When marriage is rejected as oppressive, sex is opened up to a number of possibilities, beginning with promiscuity.

In a 1986 article entitled "Remaking Love, the Real Sexual Revolution," the authors stated that given the choice between "promiscuity and repressiveness" (meaning sex confined to a long-term commitment such as marriage), many women will choose promiscuity.[50] As one woman said:

> I love the mystery of something new . . . the physical and emotional possibilities of testing myself and him. The variety *is* the turn-on.[51]

But even the variety of promiscuity can become routine. Thus, one feminist suggests that

> ... even if you have a lot of sex, you might feel like making love to yourself—every so often—or often.[52]

For the more radical feminists, however, even heterosexual promiscuity can be oppressive and the sexual options are fewer. "Women who no longer associate with men . . . have only one group left to relate to—women."[53] As a result, feminism ends up not only endorsing but promoting lesbianism. As author Joan Cassell notes:

> ... many women who are already lesbians become feminists. But in addition, a large number of women become lesbians after they become feminists.[54]

Social scientists Gerlach and Hine in their study of contemporary social movements suggest that becoming a lesbian serves as a "bridge-burning act" for a feminist. It is an overt act which separates the convert to feminism from her former life and associates.[55] Thus "the lesbian is often presented as the ultimate feminist, and the model for all others, because she is the embodiment of complete freedom from male domination."[56]

And that's not all the lesbian is free from. Extolling the "virtues" of being a lesbian, one feminist writes:

> She is freed from the fear of unwanted pregnancy and the pains of childbirth, and from the drudgery of child raising.[57]

It should not surprise us then that feminism endorses abortion.

Children and Abortion

Since in the feminist view the traditional domestic structure denies a woman "personal fulfillment," it is only consistent that children also be viewed as a hindrance to this goal. One commentator compares the passages in feminist writings on children to *Playboy* magazine's treatment of women, finding in each the "same condescension and tendency to see the child [or woman] as an object rather than a person."[58] At best, children must take a back-seat to the career of their mothers.

> It is only desirable for the child that its mother be fulfilled in her relation to society, and it can only gain from being left less to the care of its parents and more to that of adults whose relation to it is impersonal and hence pure. In a properly orga-nized community then, children would be taken in charge for the most part by the community, the mother would be cared for and helped and maternity would cease to be incompatible with careers for women.[59]

Of course, all of that presupposes the birth of children, something one should not necessarily do when dealing with feminists. One of the basic tenets of the women's movement is the principle of bodily self-determination, which underlies an emphasis on abortion.

> If women have access to abortion, they have control over when, how often, and in what context they become mothers. They can plan both their families and their careers and in so doing compete independently in the same economic market place as men. If they have no access to abortion, women are economi-cally dependent upon those who can compete freely for jobs . . . men. *Those who would ban abortion seek to reinstate a traditional family structure.*[60] (emphasis mine)

The conclusion of such testimony is rather clear: feminism as an ideology directly opposes God's purpose and design for the sexes. Feminism ultimately opposes the authority of the Word of God on the basis of its teachings on the creation of man and the relationship between the sexes. As a result, feminism denies that there is any legitimate distinction between the sexes and thereby also denies the need for sexual complementarity. Thus marriage, heterosexuality, and the traditional family can be abandoned and lesbianism and abortion affirmed. Clearly, Christians must reject the ideology of feminism and the women's movement in light of what it proposes.

This is not to say that some women do not have legitimate grievances against men. Women have a reason to be angry when men abandon them and their children, especially when they refuse to support them. Men are wrong when they abuse their positions of authority in order to satisfy their own ego needs or compensate for their own lack of self-worth. But the solution to these problems will not be found in the tenets of feminism. Instead, what is needed is a complete submission on the part of men and women to the person of Jesus Christ.

FIVE

HOMOSEXUALITY

Homosexuality is sin. The Bible declares this to be so, and we cannot "exegete" our way out of it.[1] It was sin in the Old Testament, it was sin in the New Testament, and it is still sin today. People who commit homosexual acts are sinners.

Now, having said that, let me also say this: we are not sinners because we sin; rather, we sin because we are sinners. All of us sin because it is in our nature to do so. No one can escape it—"for all have sinned and fall short of the glory of God" (Rom. 3:23). People are not born with homosexual natures; they are born with sinful natures which sometimes lead them into homosexuality.

But not all of us are homosexuals. And although we can all accept the fact that we are sinners (even though we do not always take sin as seriously as we ought), there is something that causes us to see this sin of homosexuality differently. Why do we eschew this sin unlike any other?

Perhaps it is because we tend to react to sin in much the same way we react to our wounds—in terms of their visible severity. There are scrapes and scratches which we lightly brush away, but there are also gashes and severings which leave limbs hanging, stunning our senses with shock. Of course, there is a danger in treating any wound lightly, for if the scrapes and scratches go unattended, the infection which results may wreak as much injury as a severing.

Likewise, we do not see all sin the same way. And perhaps we shouldn't. Stealing a candy bar from the supermarket certainly cannot be compared to the malicious murder of an innocent person. Cheating hundreds of elderly people out of their life's savings is surely in some way worse than cheating on an algebra exam. Similarly, the molestation of children is much more heinous than beating one's dog. Not all sin is the same.

Again, as with the wound, there is a danger in taking such a position. Sin, regardless of the severity, brings forth death if it is neglected. When we recognize that sin denigrates the very glory of God, it would seem *a priori* that any talk of a gradation or severity of sin would be unnecessary. Nevertheless, experience and more importantly Scripture itself seem to tell us otherwise. Perhaps it would be helpful to distinguish between the eternal and temporal consequences of sin. In the eternal sense all sin has one consequence—death (although there is even question whether death will be experienced the same by everyone). But on the temporal or earthly level not every sin merits the same degree of consideration. G. C. Berkouwer observes in his massive volume on sin that "it is an incontestable and universal experience that there are obvious and profound gradations of sin."[2]

Moreover, it is Scripture itself which speaks of distinctions and degrees of sin. While any attempt to minimize sin is opposed by the whole of Scripture, there are nevertheless numerous passages in the Old and New Testaments which speak of "greater" or "special" responsibility on the part of people and their sin. For example, it is "more bearable" for Sodom and Gomorrah than the city which refuses to repent (Matt. 10:15; 11:24). The slave who knew what his master wanted and did not do it is beaten more severely than the one who did not know (Luke 12:47, 48). In Hebrews 10:28, 29 a heavier penalty is meted out to those who reject the Son of God than to those who rejected the Law of Moses. With the advent of Christ, man's responsibility for sin is not lessened, but increased.

Historically both the Roman Catholic Church and the Reformation Churches have recognized a gradation of sin in their doctrine and practice. In his *Institutes of the Christian Religion*, John Calvin distinguished between private and public sins, light and grave sins, or "faults" and "shameful acts" (IV. 12, 4). While "light" sins called for rebuke, more severe discipline was necessary for "shameful acts," as we learn from the Apostle Paul.[3] In 1 Corinthians 5:15, Paul took particular exception to the aberrant sexual sin being tolerated by the church and suggested that the offender be excommunicated from the fellowship. To be sure, such action was motivated from a love to reconcile the sinner; but it does illustrate that not every sin was seen in the same way, especially since we find no other instance of redemptive banishment in Paul's dealings with other Corinthian problems.

It appears, then, that some sins do seem to have a greater degree of severity than others. The greater the harm, the grosser the perversion, or the more salacious the appetite of sin, the more we are disturbed by it. Could it be that our initial revulsion to homosexuality is not, as some have suggested, because we subconsciously fear that we might have homosexual tendencies ourselves, but rather because it is such a wanton perversion that we cannot even imagine how such a thing could come to exist?

For many this is certainly the case. I should hasten to add, however, that such a vehement view of homosexuality does not preclude the ability to have compassion for the homosexual person; nor does it necessarily prohibit one's ability to minister to the pain and needs of people who are homosexual. Does a doctor have less compassion and sense of urgency to help when he sees the severest of wounds? I would think not. Nevertheless, it is almost impossible to read many Christian treatises on homosexuality today without being made to feel guilty for viewing it as something baneful and pernicious. Instead, we are scolded for being "shocked" by such sin and are urged to "see homosexuality for what it is: a challenge to grow," and are told that we should react to it "just like any other sin" (meaning that it is more like a scrape or scratch rather than a bleeding gash or severing). Why can't we see homosexuality like "any other" sin? What makes this sin so reprehensible to our thinking?

Perhaps what disturbs our spirits more than anything else is that the sin of homosexuality results in sexual acts that not only rebel against God (as all sin does), but rebel against the natural and obvious order of creation as well. As we have already seen, in the natural order man is created as *male* and *female* intentionally designed to come together as one flesh for the purpose of procreation.

Homosexuals, however, have sexual relations with members of their own sex rather than the opposite sex. This obviously brings up several perplexities, not the least of which is how one has sexual relations with someone of the same sex. In heterosexual relationships the natural complementarity of the human anatomy clearly illustrates the design and function of male and female genitalia. God, in His marvelous creation of the human body, has so structured it that as we participate in the act of sex we can meet one another face to face—reminding us that sexual intercourse is meant to be more than a meeting of bodies—it is a meeting of persons as well. In the created order everything has its proper place and function, even the human genitalia.

But homosexual relations have no such complementarity. There is nothing to join them together as "one flesh." The homosexual's only recourse for sexual expression is when he (or she) submits himself to deviant and sexually perverted uses of the human body. Thus, the mouth and anus are grossly perverted to accommodate male genitalia; vaginas become receptacles for such "natural" objects as candles, bananas, and plastic dildos. The use of the rectum is turned from its natural function of expelling to an unnatural function of receiving any object which will fit and some that won't, including fists.

Obviously, such unnatural abuses can and do cause great damage to the body. Many homosexuals have so damaged their sphincter muscle that they are no longer able to control their bowels. Syphilus and gonorrhea of the throat are not uncommon. Is it any wonder that Paul referred to homosexuals as "abusers of themselves with mankind" (1 Cor. 6:9, KJV)?

Homosexuality not only perverts the physiology of sex; it also perverts its purpose. In the divine order of creation, sex was given to man so that he might produce *children* in the context of a *loving, committed* relationship. Generally, homosexual relationships deny all three aspects of this possibility, certainly the first. Let us look briefly at all three.

First, homosexuality denies the primary purpose of sex—namely, to produce children. God's first command to man was that he be "fruitful and increase in number; fill the earth" (Gen. 1:28). But how can a homosexual relationship participate in God's command to be fruitful? Certainly homosexuals might point to heterosexual couples and observe that many of them also cannot participate in this command, but the comparison is not the same. In the heterosexual relationship there is at least a potential and always a symbolic affirmation of God's design for human sexuality, whereas in the homosexual relationship there is neither a potential for procreation nor a symbolic affirmation of it. In the homosexual relationship the seed never finds a place where it can be fertile and fruitful; so it is either spilled or ingested, ultimately denying the purpose of God.

The second thing that homosexual relationships deny is what so many of them are desperately looking for, and that is love. This is not to say that there are not homosexuals who may feel deeply for one another; but generally speaking this is not true of most homosexual relationships, at least in the Biblical definition of love. Love, from a Biblical perspective, "is not self-seeking" (1 Cor. 13:5; see also Eph. 5:22, 25). Homosexuals primarily tend to be self-seekers.

Surely this is a bold statement (some would say bigoted), but it is not made without consideration. While it may be rightly argued that society as a whole tends to be self-seeking, formal psychological testing has revealed that homosexuals are inclined to be more emotionally dependent and narcissistic than the general population.[4] I believe there are two reasons which account for this.

First, homosexuals generally follow the same philandering pattern as the single heterosexual male. In his book *Men and Marriage* George Gilder has described this pattern as "overwhelmingly marked by lack of sustained commitment and lack of orientation toward the future."[5] Independent, moving from one sexual partner to another like sexual barbarians in search of new conquests, homosexuals, like single heterosexual men, are promiscuous, impulsive, and predatory. Consider the testimony of one homosexual who admitted, "When it comes to my sexual needs, it should begin and end with what I think of me . . . what I want for me."[6] Another put it this way:

> The homosexual life is freer. The homosexual is more independent, and independence is the most attractive aspect of homosexuality. Is that selfish? Perhaps, but I think we have reached a point in time where many people can choose to live "selfishly" rather than by the old and expected norm of "sharing" your life with a family. I do not wish to be a breadwinner. Furthermore, I do not like to have people hanging on me: I am dependent on no one and I do not wish for anyone to be dependent on me.[7]

Do such testimonies echo the sentiments of Biblical love?
Perhaps some would argue that this inclination toward selfish-

ness is more directly attributable to the fact that we are dealing with single men rather than something that is particular to homosexuals. However, unlike single men, who will most likely submit their philanderings to marriage and channel their sexual energies into creating and maintaining a family, the homosexual has no civilizing influence in his life. Even if he decides to maintain a long-term relationship, it will be with the same sex who has the same rapacious characteristics.

The second thing that causes homosexuals to be self-seeking is the nature of the perversion itself. Homosexuality almost demands a preoccupation with the self in its effort to satisfy an insatiable appetite. Its emphasis on sex and its ironic inability to have it continually require the innovation of new techniques and more bizarre variations. Realizing that there are only so many variations one can experience, even in the most perverted tangents of sexual activity, homosexuals often become bored with one another. Even those who "commit" themselves to one another for any significant length of time often cruise alone in hopes of finding "new adventure." True love satisfies because true love is based on commitment. Homosexuals are rarely satisfied because they are rarely committed.

This is, in fact, the third thing homosexuality denies in a relationship—long-term commitment. Again there are homosexual couples who are exceptions to the rule, but for the most part male homosexuals tend to seek sexual release and usually do not form lasting relationships.[8] Actually it may be more accurate to say that promiscuity runs rampant in homosexual communities. In a survey of homosexual males in San Francisco, 28 percent reported having had more than a thousand partners, and 75 percent said they had had more than a hundred partners.[9] Should we expect this from any relationship devoid of love and commitment, or is such indiscrimination peculiar to the homosexual lifestyle?

Tragically, this lack of commitment on the part of homosexuals has been largely responsible for the spread of AIDS in this country. It is estimated that 70 percent of homosexuals in New York City, one of the nation's "hot spots" for homosexual activity, carry the virus.[10] Moreover, because commitments rarely last for very long and rejection happens often, homosexuals experience tremendous loneliness. This loneliness has led many homosexuals into drug

70

addiction and alcoholism, and much too often suicide. Is it any wonder, then, that we are taken aback by homosexual sin?

But while we may be repulsed by homosexual sin, we must be careful not to reject the homosexual as a person. We must learn to make the distinction between the sin and the sinner. Yet, given the tragedy that homosexual sin brings into the lives of men and women, one wonders why anyone would pursue the homosexual lifestyle. What causes a person to become homosexual? And what allows the maintainence of such a lifestyle?

INDIVIDUAL CAUSES OF HOMOSEXUALITY

There have been numerous attempts to explain why people adopt homosexual lifestyles, but one thing is certain—people are not born homosexual. Although the most common apologetic used by homosexuals is to say, "I was born this way" or, "I can't help it" or even, "God created me this way," there is no scientific evidence linking homosexuality to genes, hormones, or any other aspect of congenital biology or heredity.

We have observed in earlier chapters that our biology exerts a profound influence on our lives. Even certain aspects of our behavior are influenced by our hormones. This had led some researchers to suggest that the level of hormones in a person will determine what sex that person is attracted to. Thus it has been supposed that high levels of male sex hormones before birth contribute to an attraction to females later in life, no matter what the genetic sex of the individual is, while low levels of male hormones contribute to an attraction for males. But research has shown that after comparing the hormone levels in extremely effeminate males, both homosexual and heterosexual, there is no difference in the level of hormones in either. In fact, some findings have uncovered an even higher ratio of male hormones in homosexuals than in heterosexuals.[11] While biology may play an important part in defining our sexuality, it does not determine a sexual preference for persons of the same sex. If it did, we might be able to describe homosexuality as a sickness, but we could not call it sin. Moreover, if it were a sickness it would be the only one which God said is worthy of eternal death (Rom. 1:32).

Most researchers are agreed that no one simple cause can explain what predisposes an individual to become homosexual. It

71

has been suggested that a variety of factors must be considered in determining the causes of homosexuality. What does seem sure after gathering the data is that if enough of these factors are present, an individual may be more inclined toward homosexuality than someone in which these components are not found. Let's consider some of the more common factors used to explain homosexual predispositions.

One factor which may predispose someone toward homosexuality is an early interest in sex accompanied by heavy masturbation. Sexual awareness usually begins at a very early age, but the energy it produces is usually diffused through the great amount of activity expended at play. Sometimes, however, this sexual energy is channeled into the practice of masturbation very early in life, for some children as young as five years old.

Sexual awareness and stimulation very early in life may have a significant impact on sexual identity. Psychologist Clarence Tripp observes:

A considerable body of data indicates that boys who begin masturbating early (usually before puberty) while simultaneously looking at their own genitalia can build a crucial associative connection between maleness, male genitalia, and all that is sexually valuable and exciting. These associations amount to an eroticism which is "ready" to extend itself to other male attributes, particularly to those of a later same-sex partner.[12]

Tripp goes on to conclude that this associative pattern sometimes manages to preempt heterosexual interests as it pursues same-sex activity. Childhood is a time of curiosity and discovery about life, including sex. Such curiosity sometimes leads to sexual experimentation, often with other boys, and may produce a receptivity to same-sex sexual activity.

Often a sexual trauma at a young age is a factor in someone moving toward homosexuality. A young girl molested by her father, an older brother, or some other older man may come to hate sex or men later in life. Many lesbians have attributed their hatred toward men as the result of a molesting father.

By contrast young boys are not usually physically molested by their mothers, which we might expect if we were to account for a rejection of preference for the opposite sex. Instead we find that boys are also molested by a father or older boy, perhaps a male baby-sitter. While such experiences can produce great guilt, they do not produce the same kind of reaction we find in adolescent girls. Instead, we often find feelings of guilt mixed with a sense of sexual stimulation and excitement at the same time, resulting in a kind of sexual confusion which may open a door to further same-sex sexual activity and homosexual predisposition.

Perhaps the most important factor in accounting for a homosexual predisposition is faulty parental relationships between the parents themselves and between the parents and child. No other relationship plays as significant and important role in influencing the life of a child as the parent-child relationship. Positive parental role models where couples respond positively to one another and to their children are more likely to produce positive, well-adjusted children than in homes where parents abdicate their roles. Consequently, negative parental relationships can have a significant impact on a child's potential sexual preference.

Psychiatrist David Busley has observed nine different patterns of parental relationships which may contribute to abnormal psychosexual development:

1. Absence of intimacy of the mother with the father.
2. The absent father . . . coupled with a mother who is too "present."
3. The punitive father coupled with a masochistic mother.
4. A passive father with a domineering mother who relates to the boy in an overly protective or overly permissive way.
5. An aloof father coupled with a mother who is too close and overly involved.
6. A vulgar father coupled with a prudish mother, giving the child an impression that masculine sexuality is reprehensible.
7. Both parents absent from the child before he is twelve.
8. The idealized mother coupled with a block in the child's identifying with the father, resulting in overidentification with the mother.
9. The idealized father (or older brother), resulting in a kind of hostile-dependency with the father.[13]

In a marriage where husbands and wives have not learned to properly relate to one another in the context of their roles, it is often the child who is victimized.

In the case where a husband and wife cannot preserve a loving relationship, the wife may channel her love and affection to her son in an unhealthy way of making him the primary object of her attention rather than her husband. This abnormal doting and smothering of the son by the mother may cause him to begin identifying more with her than with his father. The mother may unconsciously encourage feminine activities and attitudes which produce effeminate mannerisms in the son. While these mannerisms by themselves do not denote homosexuality, the process which encourages such mannerisms may leave the son more inclined toward homosexual relationships.[14]

On the other hand, a mother may be so domineering and commanding in the home that it can produce such hostility in the child against the opposite sex that he is unable to relate to other women in a normal way.

Of course, this is only possible because of the husband's passivity and lack of assertiveness. It is almost impossible to find a homosexual who has enjoyed a warm, loving relationship with his father. A statistically significant number of homosexuals in one survey said they had a bad relationship with their fathers or none at all.[15] By contrast, research has shown that "it is practically impossible for homosexuality to result in a home where the child has at least one sound relationship with either parent."[16]

Others have argued that homosexual compulsion arises from a rejection of the self often determined by paternal rejection in which one feels estranged or unaffirmed in certain attributes of his masculine personality or physical body. This unaffirmed identity gives rise to what Leanne Payne has identified as the "cannibal compulsion."[17] This theory suggests that like cannibals who eat only those they admire in order to get their traits, homosexual compulsion is a way of gaining those masculine attributes one feels he is missing in his own life.

In a similar way, Gilder maintains that a frequent catalyst of homosexuality is self-abasement.

Failure in love or work may so deject a man that he feels incapable of rising to a relationship with a woman. He may find

he lacks the confidence for the rudimentary acts of self-asser-
tion—even the rudimentary selfhood—needed for any heterosexual exchange. He becomes fixated on his own physical
limitations and begins worshiping the male members of others.[18]

Thus, a man who does not feel himself a man may seek to have a
man. Homosexual activity, according to Gilder, "does not require
confidence or male identity or a face-to-face self exposure . . . it
can even be managed without an erection. It is an inviting escape
for the fallen male."[19]

It should be clear, then, that no one cause can account for
homosexual behavior in every case. While any one of the above
factors may be influential in a person's homosexual disposition,
such components fail to explain why many children who have been
subjected to sexually traumatic experiences or who have been
reared by domineering mothers and passive fathers grow up heterosexual. This is not to say that there is no connection between such
factors; nevertheless, they cannot adequately explain all that causes
homosexuality. A predisposition toward homosexuality does not
make one a homosexual. Rather, it is a homosexual predisposition
accompanied by homosexual activity which confirms a person as
homosexual. What seems to be characteristic in all homosexual
behavior, however, is that homosexual predisposition never gives
way to homosexual activity unless there has been a feeding of the
thought-life through fantasy or pornography about same-sex experiences.

It is the resolve of the mind, stimulated through fantasy and
usually accompanied by masturbation, that may finally persuade a
person to pursue homosexual partners. Prominent in the homosexual experience is the use of pornographic material. One writer
describes the use of pornography in this way: "What is viewed is
first masturbated to at the fantasy level, then later acted out in real
life behavior."[20] When someone commits a homosexual act, it is
invariably preceded by thoughts that have been rehearsed in the
mind over and over again. Once the act is committed, it reinforces
those thought patterns which in turn begin to feed off the experience, and the mind soon becomes obsessed with homosexual fantasies.

But one of the most important observations which emerges

from this pattern is that ultimately homosexual *behavior* becomes a choice. If actions are a result of thoughts, then whatever else may predispose one toward homosexuality, it is finally what one chooses to do with his thoughts that will make the greatest difference in his sexual preference. Because we *choose* what we will feed our minds with, the strongest incentive toward homosexual behavior is also the one over which we have the most control.

No one has a choice about what kinds of sexual tragedies he will experience as a child or how his parents will relate toward each other or himself. What one can do, however, is choose what he will do with the thoughts that arise from such circumstances. This is not to say that the choice is easy; challenging the thought-life of any sexual addiction is extremely difficult. Nevertheless, while homosexual thought patterns may be deeply entrenched and addictive, our thought-life is not uncontrollable, nor is it incapable of change and redirection. (Insights for dealing with obsessive thoughts and where they are rooted can be found in Chapter Ten.)

But there is another side of the homosexual problem. While it is important to understand something about what causes an individual to choose homosexuality, it is also important to understand what reinforces that choice. Certainly not every homosexual has a desire to change either his thoughts or his lifestyle. Moreover, because it is difficult to practice a lifestyle that is discouraged by a majority of society, homosexuals have sought to gain greater acceptance by that segment of society. The full acceptance of homosexuality by society then becomes very important in maintaining the homosexual lifestyle.

THE HOMOSEXUAL MOVEMENT

Perhaps the most important event in legitimizing the maintainance of the homosexual lifestyle has been the rapid growth of the homosexual movement. In the past few years the issue of homosexuality has come out of the closet and into our living rooms. Once considered an issue too sensitive to talk about in public, it is now nearly impossible to pick up a daily paper or listen to a news broadcast without some mention of homosexuality or a related topic such as AIDS. (Despite the best efforts of the homosexual movement to convince us otherwise, AIDS is almost exclusively a homosexual disease.)

When one considers the fact that America's traditional religious beliefs have historically condemned the practice of homosexuality, and past social convention has demanded that attention given to the subject be kept to a minimum, it is evident that "a veritable revolution has taken place in the last thirty years."[21]

The homosexual movement has invaded every area of American life—from education to religion, from politics to entertainment. According to the Gay Teachers Association of New York City, there are up to ten thousand homosexual teachers in New York City alone. A number of mainline denominations not only condone the practice of homosexuality but ordain homosexuals into the ministry. Mayors and state officials march in gay-pride parades, while homosexual groups have enjoyed the support of the White House. The practice of homosexuality has been declared "normal" by the psychiatric establishment, and television programs and movies portray homosexuality as an acceptable and, at times, even desirable lifestyle. Gay student organizations are funded by the distribution of student activity fees using monies paid by nonhomosexual students or their parents to promote homosexual activities. Due to successful efforts undertaken by the Carter Administration, even the IRS recognizes homosexual organizations as "charitable" for tax purposes in the same category as hospitals, churches, and schools.[22]

But such advancements are not good enough for those in the homosexual movement, because they realize that a large segment of the American population still refuses to accept the legitimacy of homosexual behavior. The homosexual subculture recognizes that although it enjoys the acceptance of a very visible sector of society (the information elite), that acceptance is nevertheless a small cross section of America's attitudes toward homosexuality.[23] It is the everyday American whose support they must win. As Enrique Rueda states in *The Homosexual Network*, the ultimate goal of the homosexual movement can be summarized in a very simple phrase:

ACCEPTANCE OF HOMOSEXUAL ACTS AS A
NORMAL VARIANT OF HUMAN BEHAVIOR AND OF
HOMOSEXUALITY AS AN ALTERNATIVE LIFESTYLE.[24]

One magazine articulated the objective of the homosexual movement in this way:

... the ultimate objective of at least a significant segment of the movement for homosexual rights is not simply to establish legal protection for homosexuals against any discrimination based on their private lives, but also to win the eventual acceptance, on the part of both society and church, of homosexual behavior as a legitimate alternative that holds the full promise of human development and is in every way consistent with the Judeo-Christian ethical tradition.[25]

In February 1972 a National Coalition of Gay Organizations adopted what constitutes one of the most detailed outlines for societal acceptance of the homosexual lifestyle produced by the movement thus far. Included in the "1972 Gay Rights Platform" were such demands as:

—Federal encouragement and support for sex education courses, prepared and taught by Gay women and men, presenting homosexuality as a valid, healthy preference and lifestyle as a viable alternative to heterosexuality.

—Federal funding of aid programs of Gay men's and women's organizations designed to alleviate the problems encountered by Gay women and men which are engendered by an oppressive sexist society.

—Repeal of all laws governing the age of sexual consent.[26]

David Thorstad, head of the North American Man/Boy Love Association (NAMBLA) states:

The ultimate goal of the gay liberation movement is the achievement of sexual freedom for all—not just equal rights for "lesbians and gay men," but also freedom of sexual expression for young people and children. . . . [27]

The homosexual movement recognizes its goals will be unacceptable to a larger part of the heterosexual community unless certain other propositions are accepted first. Thus, a need arises to promote favorable attitudes toward homosexuals. This need is met through a number of propositions described in terms of positive affirmation and acceptance. Once these propositions are accepted by the heterosexual community, it is only a small step to accept the main goals of the homosexual movement.

The first proposition which must be accepted is the idea that *gay is good*. This message is ubiquitous in every quarter of the homosexual movement. The following resolution adopted by the North American Conference of Homophile Organizations (NACHO) reveals the ultimate purpose of the statement "gay is good":

BECAUSE many individual homosexuals, like many of the members of many other minority groups, suffer from diminished self-esteem, doubts and uncertainties as to their personal worth, and from a pervasive false and unwarranted sense of an inferiority and undesirability of their homosexual condition, and from a negative approach to that condition; *and*

BECAUSE, therefore, many individual homosexuals, like many of the members of many other minority groups, are in need of psychological sustenance to bolster and to support a positive and affirmative attitude toward themselves and their homosexuality and to have instilled into them a confident sense of the positive good and value of themselves and of their position; *and*

BECAUSE it would seem to be very much a function of the North American Homophile Conference to attempt to replace a wishy-washy negativism toward homosexuality with a firm no-nonsense positivism, to attempt to establish in the homosexual community and its members feeling of pride, self-esteem, self-confidence, and self-worth, in being the homosexuals that they are and have a moral right to be (these feelings being essential to true human dignity), and to attempt to bring to bear a countervailing influence against negative attitudes toward homosexuality prevalent in the heterosexual community; *and*

BECAUSE the Negro community has approached similar problems and goals with some success by the adoption of the motto or slogan: *Black is Beautiful*

RESOLVED: that it be hereby adopted as a slogan or motto for NACHO that GAY IS GOOD.[28]

This propaganda can be said in many ways, but the bottom line is always the positive affirmation of homosexuality. William Johnson, a minister with the United Church of Christ, sees gay liberation as "a movement of the Holy Spirit."[29] The following quotation is taken from a grammar school textbook on sex education:

. . . many homosexuals—more every year—are happy and satisfied. They hold good jobs and live successful lives. They are found in all walks of life—sports, business, the arts, science, government, and labor, to mention a few. And each year, more people feel that homosexuals have the right to live the kind of sexual lives they want as long as they do not harm or bother others. They are no more likely to be harmful to others than people who are not gay.[30]

The message coming through such statements, of course, is that "gay is good." And the message is being heard! A massive evaluation of sex education programs undertaken by the U.S. Department of Health, Education, and Welfare discovered that "students participating in these programs tended to become more accepting of homosexuality and masturbation."[31]

Associated with the proposition that "gay is good" is a counter-proposition that homophobia is an undesirable condition. "Homophobia," an expression denoting fear of homosexuals, is the term most commonly used by homosexuals to describe those who are not pro-gay. In essence the term constitutes the counterpart of "gay" and is always used in a negative context. According to Rueda, one of the arguments homosexuals insist on is that "If being 'gay' is the condition of accepting and affirming joyfully the fact that one is a homosexual, 'homophobia' means the rejection of such a condition."[32] In its need to promote the value of homosexuality, the movement considers homophobia as an irrational and hence undesirable condition. Rueda further suggests that homosexuals have tried to redefine the attitude of society toward homosexuality by describing homophobia as "an illness that has to be cured, a form of discrimination that has to be obliterated and, in the religious context, a sin that must be forgiven."[33]

Thus the homosexual movement has attempted to turn the tables in regard to how one views homosexuality. Whereas seeing homosexuality as wrong or immoral was once considered an appropriate response, such a response is now viewed as a sign of social immaturity, bigotry, or even mental illness. The only normal or acceptable response is the one that agrees with the proposition "gay is good."

The second proposition the homosexual movement would have us accept is that *homosexuality is not a matter of choice.* An almost universal theme within the homosexual movement is the idea that homosexuals are in no way responsible for being the way they are. Homosexual awareness is seen as a process of self-discovery rather than conscious choice. Despite the fact that no study or research to this time has linked homosexuality with any congenital factors, homosexuals are adamant in their insistence that their homosexuality is something they were born with. Thus, it is common to hear homosexuals justify their sexual preference with statements like: "I was born this way"; "I can't help being the way I am"; and even, "God made me this way." If homosexuality is to be regarded as morally equivalent to heterosexuality, it must be accepted as a condition homosexuals can do nothing about, not as a matter of choice. Enrique Rueda states:

> If homosexuality is determined before the age of reason, and its establishment is not dependent on early sexual experiences, the homosexual movement can count on the support of many heterosexuals who have come to believe that it is unavoidable.[34]

Implied in the proposition that homosexuality is not a matter of choice is the idea that homosexuality is not changeable. As a result, homosexuality is seen to be an integral part of personhood; that is, homosexuality is so identified with the person that it becomes his nature. The consequence of his belief, however, is not only the perception that homosexuality is unchangeable, but that it is actually wrong for a homosexual to attempt such a change.

The Word of God, of course, counters such claims. Scripture, as we saw from the beginning of this chapter, teaches us that homosexuality is sin, a fact which actually becomes good news in that it tells us that no one need be bound by the sin of homosexuality. The Bible tells us that "the blood of Jesus . . . purifies us from every sin" (1 John 1:7). Writing to the church at Corinth, the Apostle Paul confirmed the power of God to change men and women's lives:

> Do you not know that the wicked will not inherit the kingdom of God? Do not be deceived: Neither the sexually immoral . . . nor homosexual offenders . . . will inherit the kingdom of God. *And that is what some of you were.* But you were washed, you were sanctified, you were justified in the name of the Lord Jesus Christ and by the Spirit of our God. (1 Cor. 6:9-11, emphasis mine)

By God's grace, homosexuals can change—and indeed they must change. The consequences will be much too grievous should they refuse. At the individual level, practicing homosexuals have no part in the Kingdom of God. As a movement, homosexuality threatens the very foundation of society. There is no question that the homosexual movement views the traditional family as inimical to its interests. The notion that a family must involve persons of both sexes flies in the face of homosexual ideology. A workshop at a homosexual convention in Philadelphia included the following as one of its demands: "The abolition of the nuclear family because it perpetuates the false categories of homosexuality and heterosexuality."[35]

Professor Charles Rice of Notre Dame University concludes that:

> The legitimization of homosexual activity . . . is a predictable consequence of the separation of the unitive and procreative aspects of sex. So are promiscuity, pornography, divorce, abortion, etc. We have sunk to extraordinary depths in our contraceptive society. And it may be that we will bottom out only when the natural consequences of depravity become so intoler-

able as to remind us of the Lawgiver whose Law we are flouting. ". . . men with men doing shameless things and receiving in themselves the fitting recompense of their perversity" (Romans 1:27).[36]

ANDROGYNY

We are either male or female. At least we thought so until today.

A psychologist asked his seven-year-old nephew, "Is Michael Jackson a boy or a girl?" The boy thought for a moment and replied, "Both."[1]

Confused? Possibly and maybe even rightly so. Perhaps the boy's answer reveals not so much his inability to distinguish one sex from another as it reveals a keen observation about a rapidly growing trend in human sexuality—the move toward androgyny. Defined as "the merging of male *(andro)* and female *(gyne)* characteristics in one person," androgyny has emerged as the newest sexual trend in the 1980s and has created a new sexual confusion within a generation of already sexually disoriented young people.

Popularized through MTV, fashion designers, and even films, no one has done more to promote the trend toward androgyny than music superstars such as Michael Jackson, Boy George, and Prince.[2] Described as "pre-adolescent, like a Barbie doll with no genitals," pop singer Michael Jackson captured the attention of music fans that crossed the boundaries of generations.

Although Princess Margaret reportedly passed him off as "an over-made-up tart," Boy George (George Alan O'Dowd) pushed androgyny to the point where record company executives were willing to make his gender-blending persona a multimillion dollar property.[3]

Wearing eyeliner and lace, while singing the pleasures of auto-erotic sex, incest, and bisexuality, Prince (Prince Rogers Nelson) has successfully employed his androgynous image to sell pornographic rock to adolescents.

While it might be argued by some that such androgynous appeal is all done in the name of entertainment, evidence suggests that the move toward androgyny is more than mere showmanship, but carries with it the possibilities of new views of human sexuality, sex roles, and sexual activity. *Time* magazine carried a commentary addressing the new trend toward androgyny (described as the eleventh megatrend) in this way:

> In the future, we won't need the Tarzan-Jane relationships, and whether you are male or female won't matter. The appeal of cross-dressing and sexually ambivalent rock stars is that they tease people . . . with rigid ideas about sex roles, and prepare the way for more relaxed attitudes.[4]

As if traditional sex roles weren't being bombarded enough already. For the past two and a half decades the female sex role identity has been a major target for change by feminists, sexual liberals, and an entertainment industry bent on undermining and dismantling every traditional idea about sex roles, marriage, and family. From cigarette ads to prime-time sitcoms, today's woman is portrayed as an amalgamation of gorgeous wit, assertive independence, and corporate success—able to do it all with no one to thank but herself. She is hardly ever shown in what would be considered a demeaning traditional feminine role such as cooking, cleaning, or raising children. And if she is, it is only secondary to her career as a doctor, lawyer, or private detective or because she must come to the rescue of her bumbling idiot of a husband who can't boil water. Unfortunately, this image is even often promoted in the Christian community. Read the back cover of most any book written by a Christian woman and there she is: superwoman; author, popular national speaker, travels widely, head of this ministry or that, oh, and also wife and successful mother, leaving every "mediocre" homemaker pondering how she does it.

And what has been the result of this challenge to the traditional feminine sex role? One psychologist answers the question this way:

> Alas, it has produced a decade of depression and self doubt among women. God created us as sexual beings, and any

confusion in that understanding is devastating to the self-concept. Those most affected are the women who are inextricably identified with the traditional role, those who are "stranded" in a homemaking responsibility. Thus, wives and mothers have found themselves wondering, "who am I?" and then nervously asking, "who should I be?"[5]

Consequently, as the traditional roles of homemaking and motherhood are scorned and discredited, the majority of women who find themselves in those roles are left agitated and confused.

Not surprisingly, moreover, the self-doubt found in women has begun to surface in the masculine gender. It is only natural that any social movement creating confusion in one half of the population would certainly find its way to the other half. James Levine writing in *Psychology Today* observes:

After countless books about the condition of women have been published in the last decade, we are now getting a spate of studies about men. *One theme comes through loud and clear: the male is in crisis.* Buffeted by the women's movement, constrained by a traditional and internalized definition of "masculinity," men literally don't know who they are, what women want from them, or even what they want from themselves.[6]

Who is today's man and what does he do?

Does he open doors or give up his seat for a woman? Is he the provider and protector of his family when both partners work outside the home? Can he assume a position of authority and leadership in an age of liberation? Should he stay home and care for the kids while his wife goes to work? No one is quite sure.

With women being told that they can be as assertive and domineering as males and men being told that they can be as nurturing and sensitive as females, it is little wonder that a new generation finds itself in its own state of sexual confusion. Caught in a social tide of changing sex roles and gender identity, sexual distinctions are being swept away. We find society responding in two ways. One way is by reaffirming those distinctions which are in danger of being lost. George Gilder notes, for example, that when male nature is ignored or denied, it actually gives rise to a greater need for and emphasis on masculinity. As the natural play of male aggression is surrendered for the "right to cry" and as male virility is substituted for greater feminine expression, men begin to "feed on the masculinity of a few heroes—boxers, football players, rock stars, entrepreneurs, macho film and TV avengers."[7]

> The result is a society that at once denies the existence of natural male aggressiveness and is utterly preoccupied with it. While academic intellectuals and media sociologists ruminate on the feminized "new man," male aggression and violence, muscle and madness, guns and technologies animate our movies, TV shows, magazines, newspapers, politics, music. From Patton to Bond to Rocky to Rambo to Conan the Barbarian and scores of imitators—from Mick Jagger to Bruce Springsteen—the popular culture reeks and reverberates with male aggression. From hijacker threats to guerrilla terror, our public life revolves around male violence. Our city streets quail before it. Our city schools are paralyzed in fear of it. . . . All the while, most academic theorists maintain that men could be mild and maternal if somehow "the culture" would socialize them like women.[8]

The other response to the uncertainty surrounding sex roles and gender distinctions is simply to ignore the validity of gender distinctions altogether. After all, if sex roles are reversible and if sexual distinctions are artificial and dispensable, why continue to maintain them? Androgyny thus begins to emerge as the synthesis of sexual confusion in society. And begin to surface it has, insidiously perhaps, but androgyny is the trend of the eighties. When asked about her bisexuality, recording artist and actress Grace Jones stated:

> Women are attracted to me and I'm attracted to women as well. I am androgynous. We all are. I've just developed mine. I've been this way for years, but I think the 80's have finally caught up with Grace Jones.[9]

Have the eighties indeed caught up with Grace Jones? And what about the rest of society? From fashion to office politics to professional sports to personal lifestyles, androgyny is shaping our society. Perhaps the most obvious signals of where American culture is sexually comes through fashion. In her article, "Dressed to Thrill: The Cool and Casual Style of the New American Androgyny," Anne Hollander states:

> Dramatically perverse sexual signals are always powerful elements in the modern fashionable vocabulary, and the most sensational component among present trends is something referred to as androgyny.[10]

Until recently the way we dress has always underscored our sexual distinctiveness. Anthropologist Liza Dalby acknowledges that we have a long tradition of masculine and feminine dressing that parallels our deep notions of maleness and femaleness.[11] This probably has its origins in the law of the Old Testament where women were instructed not to wear men's clothing and men were not to wear women's clothing—such cross-dressing was detestable in the eyes of the Lord (Deut. 22:5). Such cross-dressing was detestable in the eyes of the Lord because it disregarded the distinctions between the sexes established at creation. For this reason, crossover clothing, hairstyles, and makeup make not just a fashion statement but a social and theological statement as well. And nothing makes a bigger impact in this area than androgyny.

What may have been meant to tweak middle-class morality in its beginnings—frosted hair, eyeliner, and earrings on men, for example, and ultra-short hair, neckties, and Calvin Klein jockey and boxer shorts (with the fly) for women—are now accepted as part of everyday fashion.

Androgyny, of course, goes deeper than fashion and crossover dressing. Fashion simply reflects what is happening at a deeper level of society.

The real peril of androgyny is not that men are trying to be women or women men, but that sexuality remains ambiguous—it is neither and both. Grace Jones tells us that "you can be a boy, a girl, whatever you want."[12] Joanne Smith, owner of Boy/Girl, a unisex boutique in Beverly Hills, adds, "We all have male/female qualities, why not be able to show both."[13] Even Boy George, often erroneously called a transvestite (usually understood as a man who dresses in women's clothing for sexual arousal), is not trying to fool anyone into thinking he is a girl—his name makes that point explicitly.

When it comes to androgyny, there is a definite indefiniteness to it all. Gender distinctions are deliberately blurred, creating an illusion of a sexless humanity which is neither male nor female.

Although the idea of the androgyne is an ancient one dating back to Plato's *Symposium*, for modern sex theorists the present trend toward androgyny presents itself as something of an innovation in human sexuality. Certainly it was not by coincidence that during the sexual revolution of the seventies social scientists began looking for new models of sexuality to explain human sexual behavior. With premarital sex already an accepted norm and homosexuality and the feminist movement gaining momentum, traditional sex roles were being attacked by a new breed of sexologists. And the point of attack was aimed at sexual distinctions, leaving the unisex or androgynous ideal as the most promising alternative. In their anxiety to be a part of the iconoclastic avant-garde, social scientists often seem all too willing to ignore the obvious in favor of accepting the ridiculous.

Thus, while any kindergarten teacher could have told them that there are innate differences between males and females, many social scientists weren't buying it. Why? A partial answer lies in the assumptions or presuppositions supporting the constructs of sexual theory. Two basic assumptions ran through the liberal halls of American academia and intellectualism which steered the way for rejecting gender distinctions and dismantling traditional sex roles. The first assumption was the widely accepted notion that man was capable of answering his own questions on the basis of science alone, which of course led to an outright rejection of God and the Bible. The second assumption was that if sex roles could be changed they *ipso facto* should be changed.

The first assumption was ultimately determinative for any new constructs of sexual theory, in that underlying every new theory of sexuality was a philosophical presupposition which rejected the authority of the Word of God and replaced it with humanism. Since traditional sex roles and gender distinctions were affirmed in the Biblical account of man's creation as male and female and in its subsequent teaching on marital relationships, they were not considered as having any valid bearing on a modern understanding of human sexuality. One college textbook entitled *Human Sexuality* states:

> An emphasis on scientific answers to human problems has probably undermined traditional religious approaches and beliefs in an absolute standard of morality. The shift from absolutism to relativism actually began in the nineteenth century, with the evolutionary theories of Charles Darwin. In addition, science tempers our notions of what should be by providing us with information about what is.[14]

While droves of university students across America were rejecting the traditional sexual values of their Judeo-Christian heritage in pursuit of a new existential hedonism ("if it feels good, do it!"), the way had already been paved by their professors who debunked Biblical authority as being incompatible with the modern scientific mind. Once Biblical authority had been undermined, statements in Scripture which affirm sex roles or distinctions between men and women were easily dismissed as misogynistic or culturally irrelevant.

The second assumption was that if sex roles were changing, it was because they were no longer adequate to meet the needs of a sexually informed society, and therefore sex roles *ought* to change in order to conform to that society. And what were the sexual scientists proposing to replace traditional sex roles? Proclaiming traditional sex role distinction as "unsatisfactory" and "dysfunctional," another college textbook tells us that many theorists began to view androgyny as a "highly desirable, even ideal, state of being."[15]

How does one reach this "ideal" state of being, and what are its results?

In answering the question of how we become androgynous, author June Singer tells us:

> The answer to this question is that we do not become androgynous; we already are . . . it is not necessary to learn how.[16]

Singer goes on to explain that the reason people don't experience their androgyny to the fullest is because they have been imprisoned by sex and gender. Instead of learning how one becomes androgynous, one must make it a matter of *unlearning* traditional sex role concepts. This is not easily done. Singer warns us that the world has been so entrenched in gender stereotypes that if we are to be truly free from our masculine and feminine identities we must be willing to expunge ourselves from any tradition which affirms the distinctions of the sexes. Consequently, the Judeo-Christian tradition is anathema to the Androgynous Ideal.[17]

Singer argues that traditional sex roles were simply conventions which arose in societies that needed to perpetuate themselves through the production of numerous offspring. But because this is no longer true of modern society (the old "overpopulation" phobia again), human beings should release themselves from the "boundaries of sex and gender."[18]

But in order to free themselves from the "boundaries" of sex and gender, proponents of androgyny realize that they must also release themselves from their own biology. Researchers Alexandra Kaplan and Mary Anne Sedney note this necessity in their book *Psychology and Sex Roles, an Androgynous Perspective.*

> The possibility that biological features may bear on one's behavior might seem to threaten a psychology of androgyny. If biology can influence behavior, *and if there are biological sex differences,* might that not mean that the body places limits on one's capacity for androgyny? Does the existence of biological differences between the sexes suggest that men and women are constitutionally geared to respond in sex-linked ways? Indeed, if the answer to these questions were yes, people's potential for androgynous development might need to be reevaluated.[19] (emphasis mine)

What do they mean *if* there are biological sex differences? This is a prime example of what I meant above when I said that it seems the social scientist has a knack for overlooking the obvious! The fact of the matter is that there *are* biological differences between the sexes and further, as we saw in Chapter Two, those biological differences can and do influence behavior. But this doesn't stop the theorists of sexuality. Our authors go on to say:

> . . . the fact that biology may influence behavior does not have to signal limitations on response potential. Biology can also be

seen as only one of several conditions that influence behavior, with its final role determined by interaction with environment.[20]

Now the fact that we are affected by our environment is certainly without question. We are not simply the products of our biological natures; rather, we are the products of nature and nurture. That is why the Bible stresses that we do not leave our children to the process of nature alone, but we are instructed to "train" or nurture a child in the way he should go (Prov. 22:6). That is why Scripture instructs the older women to "*train* the younger women to love their husbands and children, to be self-controlled and pure, to be busy at home, to be kind, and to be subject to their husbands" (Titus 2:4, 5).

It is true that sex roles must be taught, but this does not dismiss us from the influence of biology. Again, as we saw in Chapter Two, God has created us in such a way that our sex roles are complementary to our biological sex. Our physiological maleness and femaleness do affect our personalities and cause us to experience life in different ways. Advocates of androgyny, of course, disagree. Rather than viewing sexuality as being complementary to our biology, it seems that sexuality should be subject to an ever-changing environment divorced from the authority of God's Word. So where does biology fit, in the androgynous scheme of things?

Dr. Robert Pielke maintains that

biological sex should not be a basis for judgments about the appropriations of gender characteristics.[21]

In other words, males need not necessarily feel they must exhibit masculine characteristics, nor should women necessarily exhibit feminine characteristics. The fact that I feel or act masculine does not arise from the fact that I am a biological male, but becuase I have been taught to feel and act that way. One author goes so far as to say that even when we speak of "feminine" or "masculine" character traits, it only calls attention "to the lie that these traits are, in truth, more natural and more desirable in one sex than in the other."[22]

Masculine traits in males and feminine traits in females are now considered lies devised to perpetuate outworn sexual distinctions and thereby affirm traditional sex roles and partiarchal rule. But what to do with what have traditionally been considered masculine traits in men and feminine traits in women presents itself as something of a problem to the advocates of androgyny. While androgyny suggests the elimination of the sexual stereotyping of human character, it is in itself formulated in terms of the very concepts of masculinity and femininity which it urges to abandon. So observes Mary Anne Warren in her article "Is Androgyny the Answer to Sexual Stereotyping?":

> Is it not at least mildly paradoxical to urge people to cultivate both "feminine" and "masculine" virtues, while at the same time holding that virtues ought not be sexually stereotyped? Would it not be simpler just to say that rationality, courage, and so forth are not masculine traits in any legitimate sense of the term, in spite of the traditional presumption to the contrary? To go on calling those traits "masculine" even in the process of urging women to develop them, seems to risk encouraging the assumption that it is, after all, easier and more natural to do so.[23]

But despite the seeming unnaturalness of urging one sex to adopt the character traits of the other, androgynists refuse to maintain that there are any innate gender differences between the sexes. Advocates maintain that as traditional gender traits are rejected and sex roles are "unlearned," the possibility is opened to major changes in human personality. Joyce Trebilcot writes:

> . . . androgyny may, in the long run, lead to major changes in human attributes. It is often suggested that the androgyne is a person who is feminine part of the time and masculine part of the time. But such compartmentalization might be expected to break down, so that feminine and masculine qualities would influence one another and be modified. Imagine a person who is at the same time and in the same respect both nurturant and mastery-oriented, emotional and rational, cooperative and competitive, and so on.[24]

Certainly we can imagine men who understand how to be nurturing, emotional, and cooperative and women who can be assertive, rational, and competitive. In fact, men who do not show some degree of those traits are nothing less than barbarians, and a woman without assertiveness may have extremely low self-esteem. I would not wish to imply that men should only exhibit what have traditionally been considered masculine character traits to the degree that they cannot be sympathetic, compassionate, and so on. To be totally masculine or feminine to the exclusion of other traits is not good for social development or mental health. I would maintain, however, that men will have constant traits that are more predominant in them than in women and vice versa. These traits help us maintain our gender identity and complementary sex roles.

It is difficult to imagine what Trebilcot means when she asks us to envision a person who is at the same time and to the same degree both nurturant and mastery-oriented or cooperative and competitive without somehow losing or changing the meaning of the terms. This difficulty is certainly what she must have in mind when she writes that

> . . . androgyny in the long run may lead to an integrating of femininity and masculinity that will yield attributes, new kinds of personalities. The androgyne at this extreme would perhaps be not part feminine and part masculine, but neither feminine nor masculine, a person in whom the genders disappear.[25]

And what happens when gender disappears? The same thing that happens every time society tries to ignore or reject the distinctions between the sexes: heterosexuality, marriage, and the family are abandoned in favor of homosexuality and other perversions. Naturally androgynists view such possibilities as beneficial to society. Dr. Robert Pielke writes:

> . . . there is every reason to believe that an androgynous society would actually enhance sexuality. . . . Since the traditional sex roles (gender) have served to *restrict* the sex drive in every conceivable way, their removal would inevitably serve to encourage a much freer and more abundant sex life than ever before.[26]

And how much freer does androgynous liberation make us? Certainly not in any way condoned by Scripture. June Singer argues that "androgyny has the power to liberate the individual from the confines of the appropriate."[27] Sexual theorist Ellen Cook adds that in the androgynous lifestyle "variations from the old standards for the sexes could be seen as . . . normal, and even desirable."[28] If, then, in the traditional view of human sexuality, sexual complementarity between men and women is fundamental to appropriate sexual expression, androgyny would eliminate such a view in favor of such variations as homosexuality and masturbation, which do not depend on sexual complementarity. This is explicitly stated by Mary Anne Warren:

> Far from implying that homosexual relationships are in some way inferior, androgynism undermines one of the primary rationales for heterosexuality— i.e., the notion that a viable sexual relationship requires that the parties be of different sexes in order that the "masculine" virtues of the one may complement the "feminine" virtues of the other. Androgynism places the complementary virtues within each individual, thus obviating this particular reason for seeking sexual union only with persons of the opposite sex. It is also reasonable to predict that to the extent that the old stereotypes are replaced by an androgynous ideal of human character, lesbianism and male homosexuality will cease to be so deeply stigmatized, because they will no longer be associated with "manishness" in women or "effeminacy" in men.[29]

Notice the important shift which has taken place in the above paragraph. There is no longer any need to acknowledge the complementarity between the sexes because complementarity is now moved to within each individual, voiding any need for the opposite sex. Sex, therefore, is divorced from procreation and especially the mutual sharing of one's being through the intimacies of sexual commitment. Sex is simply a mechanistic means for physical self-gratification, and how the sexual appetite is fed is of little concern. With each person complete in himself, all that is needed for sexual fulfillment is genital stimulation. Thus, not only is the need for the opposite sex no longer required for sexual encounter—there is ultimately no need for other people at all when it comes to sexual fulfillment. Masturbation is thus promoted as the means for sexual fulfillment.

June Singer described masturbation as an "inner resource" that may be drawn up as part of the sexual repetoire of the androgyne.[30]

> Masturbation can be seen as the expression of an urge toward the independence of an individual from other people as well as from an authoritarian God image. . . . [31]

While Singer doesn't describe how men and women should intereact with one another, one thing is certain: any sexual reciprocity between them is not necessary. Although she is not entirely adverse to sexual relationships with other people (male or female), it is important that independence and sexual autonomy be maintained.

Masturbation is thus an important vehicle not only for sexual satisfaction, but for maintaining one's independence as well. She writes:

> There is great freedom in knowing that one can be whole in one's inner life, and that this wholeness need not depend absolutely upon a relationship with another person. . . . What is important is that if one is open to the possibility of masturbation and to the value of masturbation, then a sexual relationship with another person becomes a matter of choice rather than necessity. . . . The alternative is a relationship that is less free because the need for each other is so crucial. . . .
> The androgyne knows that "being one's own person" includes the freedom of doing many things—not the least of which is being one's own lover.[32]

In the end, androgyny may reflect the ultimate form of idolatry in that one's self commands the greatest focus of love and attention. What happens when one is one's own lover? Personal fulfillment is grossly overemphasized and attention to sex roles, marriage, and family are minimized. People become objects used to meet one's own needs, deemphasizing the importance of personal relationships. Such "freedom" as Singer advocates can only lead to loneliness and despair.

Freedom cannot come in the denial of our sexual complementarity or the pursuit of the androgynous ideal—a humanity that is neither male nor female. The quest to transcend our sexual distinctions in the hope of creating some new order of "true humanity" that is not bound by gender or sex roles is at best quixotic.

Ultimately we must realize that humanity is made up of individuals, and individuals are either male or female. True humanity is recognizing that God has created each of us as one or the other and living our lives in congruence with God's design and purpose for our sexuality.

SEVEN

PORNOGRAPHY

THE LAW OF DIMINISHING RETURN

*M*s. Cosmopolitan greets us at the supermarket checkout stand each month without a smile. She speaks with beautiful almond eyes captured in a sensuous glance that seems to say to every woman, "I'm the woman you'd love to be" and to every man who looks her way, "I'm the woman you'd love to have." Her low-cut blouse lures us to her partially-bared breasts, and she lets us stare. She is the desire of every man and the model for every woman.

Tempting, sensuous, and sophisticated, she is truly the cosmopolitan woman. But is she pornographic? Despite her sex appeal, *most* would probably say no. We are curious but not aroused. By the time we have paid for the Pampers and pretzels, she's gone.

Across town at a magazine checkout stand someone is meeting Miss November. She is just as pretty, but much more friendly than Ms. Cosmopolitan. She lets me know she wants me. In fact, she invites me to take her home where she can show herself, all of herself, just to me. She undresses so I can see her perfect body, and she lets me know that I could have her anytime I want. On every glossy page I'm aroused and excited. But is she pornographic? *Many* would probably say yes, although by law she is not obscene. And every month we can meet her friends, who are equally beautiful and just as willing to give themselves to us.

And in a different part of town still, someone is looking at Lisa. She is not glamorous and not really pretty. Although she too is scantily dressed, she has no teasing breasts to bare, for Lisa is only ten years old. She is pictured in a thirty-two-page, two-color magazine holding a male dachshund in her arms. Inside the cover Lisa is shown in twenty-nine graphic displays which depict her in acts of masturbating the dog, exposing her prepubescent genitalia to her dog, and laying on her stomach as the dog mounts her from behind.[1] Pornographic? Horrifyingly so. We find ourselves sickened by the thought of such obscene and abusive acts, and they do not quickly leave our minds.

It is apparent that pornographic material is not all the same. It comes to us in varying degrees of explicitness and perversion, from "soft porn" nudity to "hard core" sexual violence and degradation, and most of us do not seem to have a great deal of difficulty recognizing it, especially in cases like Lisa above, where we feel shame and rage welling up within us. Perhaps we cannot define it, but like the late Supreme Court Justice J. Stewart, we know it when we see it. Somehow we are able to recognize when a line is crossed that makes something pornographic. And somehow we feel something ought to be done about it.

All of this, however, is not very helpful from a legal point of view. Legally, only what is considered obscene is unprotected by the First Amendment. Moreover, not all pornography is considered obscene. Therefore, what most of us would recognize as pornographic can be sold and distributed under First Amendment protection.

But even the task of legally defining what is obscene has proven to be next to impossible. In the 1957 *Roth v. United States* case, the Supreme Court defined obscenity as that which is "utterly without redeeming social importance . . ." and which ". . . deals with sex in a manner appealing to prurient interests." Again, in 1966 obscene material was defined as that which was "utterly without redeeming social value." And in the 1973 case *Miller v. California*, the Supreme Court declared that material was obscene if it met *all* of the three following conditions:

1. The average person, applying contemporary community standards, would find that the work taken as a whole, appeals to prurient interest (in sex); and

2. the work depicts or describes, in a patently offensive way,

sexual conduct specifically defined by the applicable state (or federal) law; and

3. the work taken as a whole, lacks serious literary, artistic, political, or scientific value.[2]

Needless to say, almost every word in the Supreme Court's definitions has been taken to task. Words like "utterly," "taken as a whole," or "patently offensive" are so broad that there is very little which can be shown to have *no* value at all. The smart publisher of pornographic material simply includes a political phrase or cartoon and this validates the material. Interpretation of the law is so subjective that anything might be considered permissible. Moreover, what the "average person, applying contemporary community standards," might find obscene is certainly subject to change, especially in a culture given over to a "depraved mind" (Rom. 1:28) which has no absolute standard to which to appeal. Thus, for example, in our American culture publications such as *Playboy*, *Penthouse*, or *Hustler* might be considered pornographic, but by law they are not obscene, and thus are granted protection under the rights of the First Amendment. This despite the fact that it has been shown that all three of these magazines portray sex between children and adults through cartoons or through photographs of adults dressed to suggest children.[3] What this means according to psychologist David A. Scott

. . . is that magazines can escape the letter of child pornography laws while still implying that sex with children is desirable and readily available. And these magazines, of course, are sold in the open.[4]

But while the subterfuge over legal definitions goes unsettled, the pornography industry continues to grow, both in its distribution and in its perversity.

Reaping yearly profits of over eight billion dollars, pornographic material produces a cash revenue equal in profits with the Hollywood film and record industry combined. More profits are made from pornography in Los Angeles alone than Sears & Roebuck, the nation's leading retailer, makes nationwide.[5]

There are currently some seven hundred "adults only" pornographic theaters in the United States. Selling an estimated two million tickets each week, these theaters brought in five hundred million dollars in annual box office receipts in 1985.[6] Even so, many of these X-rated theaters are closing down as the video cassette recorder opens up a whole new market to the American public. Cheaper to make than films, 70 percent of the porn industry's profits are generated by the sale of video cassettes. Nearly seventeen hundred new pornographic videos were released in 1985. Some 40 percent of the nation's twenty million VCR owners bought or rented X-rated video cassettes in 1984.[7]

Even the telephone is being used as Dial-A-Porn customers pay as much as thirty-five dollars a call to engage in sexually explicit conversations or recorded phone messages. Pacific Bell estimates that their company earned twelve million dollars from Dial-A-Porn calls between October 1984 and October 1985.[8] During one day in 1983, eight thousand calls were placed to one sexually explicit recorded message service.[9]

Concomitant with this proliferation of pornographic materials has been its growing depictions of every conceivable sexual perversion and violence. Pornography has plummeted so low in its portrayal of sex that there is virtually no sexual act that has not been committed on man or beast. Psychologist Dr. James Dobson, a commissioner on the 1985 Attorney General's Commission on Pornography, warns us of the deteriorated state of an already reprobate industry in an effort to stir people into action. Although explicit (he could have been more so), he is worth quoting at length.

X-rated movies and magazines today feature oral, anal, and genital sex between women and donkeys, pigs, horses, dogs, and dozens of other animals. In a single sex shop in New York City, there were forty-six films and videos available which featured bestiality of every type. Other offerings focused on so-called "bathroom sports" including urination (golden showers), defecation, eating feces and spreading them on the face and body, mutilation of every type (including voluntary amputation), fishhooks through genitalia, fists in rectums, mousetraps on breasts, and (forgive me) the drinking of ejaculate in champagne glasses. . . . The magazines in sex shops are organized on shelves according to topic, such as Gay Violence, Vomitting, Rape, Enemas, and topics that I cannot describe even in a frank discussion of this nature.[10]

Dobson goes on to describe how his knees buckled and tears came to his eyes as hundreds of photographs were presented to the Commission depicting "pitiful boys and girls with their rectums enlarged to accommodate adult males and their vaginas penetrated with pencils, toothbrushes, and guns."[11]

Certainly such tragedies cannot occur without causing harm to those who view it, their families, and society as a whole. Although not all pornography is of the same kind, many professional people who deal with the victims of pornography believe there is "already enough evidence to indict pornography as a public health menace."[12] One of the valuable contributions of the Attorney General's Commission on Pornography was its examination of pornography's harm according to five different categories.[13] They can be summarized as follows:

SEXUALLY VIOLENT MATERIAL

This is material which contained actual or simulated sexually explicit violence, such as sadomasochistic themes which included the use of whips and chains and other instruments of torture. It also included the predominant theme of a man making sexual advance to a woman, being rejected, and then raping her until she becomes sexually aroused by this forced activity and begs for more. It also includes violent, R-rated "slasher" films which depict disfigurement or murder often accompanied by sex and nudity, such as *The Texas Chainsaw Massacre*, *The Toolbox Murders*, and *I Spit on Your Grave*.

The Commission found that there is a causal (not *casual*, as has been misquoted by the media) relationship between exposure to sexually violent materials and aggressive behavior toward women (p. 39). Furthermore, these materials lead to a greater acceptance of the "rape myth"—that is, the idea that women enjoy being forced into sexual activity and that they enjoy being physically hurt in the process. Thus, the man who sexually forces himself on a woman is simply giving the woman what she really wants, even though she may deny it (p. 40). This kind of material also fosters the attitude that victims of rape are more responsible for the assault than the rapist.

NONVIOLENT MATERIALS DEPICTING DEGRADATION, DOMINATION, SUBORDINATION, OR HUMILIATION

The studies of Dr. Dolph Zillmann define this class of pornographic material as that which portrays women as "masochistic, subservient, socially non-discriminating nymphomaniacs" (p. 41). It is the most prominent and commercially available material. A common theme in this kind of pornography is that of a man sitting atop or standing above a woman and ejaculating into her face while the woman "pleasurably" ingests the sperm.[14] Psychotherapist David Scott remarks that while these acts are not violent, they are degrading, and "the potential for lasting effects on the audience is a growing matter of concern."[15]

It has been shown that this kind of material has a "substantially similar" impact on persons as that of the violent material. Again, significant exposure to material of this variety serves not only to lessen the viewer's sympathy toward rape victims, but tends to hold victims of rape more responsible for the offense than the actual perpetrator. Substantial exposure also increases the idea that women like to be coerced into sexual activity and that the woman who says "no" really means "yes" (p. 42). The conclusion of the Commission was that nonviolent pornographic material increased the likelihood that viewers would commit rape and other acts of sexual violence on the population so exposed (p. 42).

NONVIOLENT AND NONDEGRADING MATERIALS

The amounts of material available in this category are comparatively quite small. They are defined as materials in which participants were heterosexual and consenting to have vaginal intercourse "devoid of actual or apparent violence or pain" (p. 43).

While the sex depicted in this kind of material might be considered normal, the fact that it is commercialized through publication changes its character from something that is understood by virtually all societies to be private into something public, and may thus be considered harmful just by virtue of its being shown (p. 44). Moreover, the report adds:

It is far from implausible to hypothesize that materials depicting sexual activity without marriage, love, commitment or affection bear some causal relationship to sexual activity without
marriage, love, commitment, or affection. There are undoubt-
edly many causes for what used to be called the "sexual revolution," but it is absurd to suppose that depictions or descriptions
of uncommitted sexuality were not among these. (p. 44)

Indeed, the increase in the divorce rate, teen pregnancies, and
abortions in the years since pornography has become widely available seems to confirm this statement.

NUDITY

No one on the Commission felt that the human body or its
portrayal was harmful, although it was agreed that such a statement
was somewhat of an oversimplification (p. 46). It was recognized
that nudity may be represented in a wide variety of materials
"without force, coercion, sexual activity, violence, or degradation,"
while still containing a provocative element.

The Report also noted that legitimate questions still exist about
when and how children should be exposed to nudity, nudity in
public display, and questions about when nudity stops being "mere"
nudity and as such takes on the "connotations of sexual activity" (p.
45).

THE SPECIAL HORROR OF CHILD PORNOGRAPHY

In a special chapter dealing with child pornography, the Commission wrote that "what is commonly referred to as 'child pornography' is not so much a form of pornography as it is a form of
sexual exploitations of children" (p. 66). Actual children, some as
young as one week old, are photographed while engaged in sexual
activity with adults, other children, or animals. Child pornography
therefore necessarily involves the sexual abuse of real children (p.
66).

When the 1982 Supreme Court approved of child pornography
laws on the basis of child sexual abuse, the commercial industry
was curtailed substantially. But while little or no child pornography
can be found in adult bookstores, it is nevertheless a thriving
cottage industry run by child abusers themselves. Moreover, there

also appears to be a substantial foreign commercial network that flows into the United States almost untouched through the mail (p. 67).

Since the possibility of consent is considered an impossibility, the harm which accompanies child sexual activity is extraordinarily serious. In addition to the severe physical and psychological damage done to the child under the circumstances in which sexual photographs are made, a permanent record of these nonconsensual sexual practices can follow a child through adulthood, resulting in embarrassment and humiliation (p. 68).

Furthermore, photographs of children engaged in sexual activity are often used as tools in the process of molestation. Such photographs are shown to children to convince them that if pictures were made of other children engaged in sexual activity, it must be all right for them to do so also.

It is estimated that between six hundred thousand and one million two hundred thousand children are sexually abused and drawn into the world of child pornography every year, although estimates vary because experts believe that 50 percent or more of child sexual abuse cases are never reported.[16] Tragically, there are now organizations which openly advocate the sexual abuse of children. There are now over 280 magazines dedicated to "kiddie" porn. The California-based Rene Guyon Society, which boasts 8,500 members, promotes the motto "sex by eight or it's too late." The North American Man/Boy Love Association, active in eleven major cities, advocates that the age of consensual sexual activity between adults and children be abolished altogether.[17]

It seems that the growth of pornography in sheer volume and its steady movement toward greater violence, degradation, and perversion should tell us something about the nature of pornography—and I believe that it does.

There is abundant evidence which indicates that for many, the use of pornography is both progressive and addictive in nature. Pornography succumbs to the Law of Diminishing Return. In other words, the more one exposes himself to sexually explicit material, the less he "gets" out of it, and so he must continually increase "the dosage" in order to achieve the same amount of stimulus and excitation.

Research by social psychologist Dr. Dolf Zillmann at Indiana

University and later replicated by Dr. James Check at York University and Dr. Gene Abel at Emory Univeristy found that people who are bored by ordinary pornography develop a lust for stronger, more perverted versions.[18] Zillmann concluded:

> Persons are suddenly dissatisfied with what they are so familiar with. There seems to be an indication that they are now ready to go for more. The usual is no longer good enough, and there has to be more. And this "more," of course, means bizarre sex or violent sex.[19]

The question is, how much worse can it get? How much worse will we allow it to get?

It seems only logical that the individual who exposes himself to pornography exposes himself to the values it communicates. Eventually he will accept those values inherent in pornography's message and oppose those values pornography opposes. As more individuals in a society give themselves to the grip of pornography, the more pornography will grip society. Should society as a whole ever adopt the values of pornography, it will oppose the very existence of society itself. Even now it opposes everything God has declared as good. And what is that?

Pornography Opposes God

God, Jesus Christ, and the Christian church have traditionally been the targets of blasphemous pornographic jokes and articles. Pornography often depicts Jesus as a promiscuous homosexual.

In opposing God, pornography opposes God's creation. God has created man in His own image, unique and distinctly accountable to his Creator. By contrast, pornography portrays man as a biological urge totally unaccountable to anyone but himself. God designed sex to be between male and female with a procreative purpose. Pornography rejects sexual distinctions and indeed even human distinctions. Its promotion of homosexuality and bestiality, along with its emphasis on oral and anal intercourse, either prohibits or denies God's purpose of procreative sex.

God has designed sexual intercourse to take place with one's partner in the context of marriage. Pornography, on the other hand, rejects marriage and promotes sexual activity between a variety of partners. God has designed sex as an expression of love, while pornography treats it as an expression of lust.

Pornography Opposes Marriage

The most common theme of pornography according to one researcher is this: "strangers meet. They look each other over. They are overcome with sexual desire. He is ready to take. She is ready to be taken. . . ."[20] What then follows are the *standard* portrayals of sexual activity, including oral and anal intercourse. In addition, more than half of this material features a third or fourth party, including group sex. The message is that sexual activity has little to do with intimacy or lifetime commitment in raising a family.

The research of Zillmann and Bryant concluded that exposure to this kind of pornography clearly makes people more likely to believe that:

—The greatest sexual joy comes without enduring commitment.
—Partners expect each other to be unfaithful.
—There are health risks repressing sexual urges.
—Promiscuity is natural.
—Children are liabilities and handicaps.[21]

Thus pornography cuts at the very fabric of which marriage is made—commitment, trust, faithfulness, and the fruit of marriage: children.

Not only does exposure to pornography affect attitudes *toward* marriage; it also affects attitudes *in* marriage. Contrary to popular belief, viewing pornography does not enhance the quality of sex in marriage. It has been shown that people actually become more disenchanted with their partners and sexual activity when they compare them with the orgiastic exploits and perfect airbrushed bodies portrayed in pornographic material.

Again, research by Zillmann and Bryant discovered that:

—Exposure to pornography diminished satisfaction with the physical appearance of the respondent's sexual partner.
—It reduced satisfaction with the partner's affection, sexual behavior, and sexual curiosity and innovations.

—It reduced the overall satisfaction with the respondent's present intimate relationship.

—It enhanced the importance of sex without emotional involvement.[22]

What is apparent is that pornography promotes the need to fulfill one's own fantasies and selfish needs without regard or concern for one's partner. It therefore stands in opposition to marriage.

Pornography Opposes Children

Not only are children tragically exploited as victims of sexual abuse and molestation, but there is a bias against their very existence. Since pornographic sex is totally disssociated from procreative sex, children are seen as unwanted accidents, liabilities, and handicaps.

Pornography also threatens children's environments. The biggest fear among elementary students is the fear of being kidnapped or molested. This fear accompanies them everywhere they go from the school playground to their own front yards.

Pornography Opposes the Future

Implied in the fact that pornography opposes children is the fact that the future, which is dependent on children, is of little consequence. Pornographic sex is a totally existential expression of lust without regard to its consequences. Any connection to the future through children is purely accidental.

Pornography Opposes Women

Most pornography humiliates and degrades women. They are the usual victims of rape, beatings, and torture—simply sex objects to be used and abused by men. Pornography denies women their most important roles as wife and mother.

Pornography Opposes Authentic Humanity

By its preoccupation with physical anatomy, genitalia, and the pursuit of personal sexual gratification, pornography portrays sex in a way that is disssociated with the meeting of persons. Much of the sexual activity that occurs in pornography makes it physically impossible for the partners to meet one another face to face. Certainly the viewer of the material has no contact with real persons. More dehumanizing still is the portrayal of sex with animals "as if they could be simply another variety of human experience."[23]

Pornography Opposes Society

There is now no doubt that pornography contributes to a callousness toward rape and a desensitization toward violence. Pornography *does* have a causal effect on sexual violence and aggression in the community.

Moreover, pornography is closely linked with syndicated crime. Organized crime now controls more than 85 percent of all commercially produced pornography.[24] Tightly connected to the porn industry is organized crime's control of drugs and prostitution.

Finally, pornography pollutes our environment. It fills our airways with rock lyrics that blatantly promote mutual masturbation, incest, oral sex, and even necrophylia (sex with the dead).[25] It comes into view on our newsstands and on our televisions—*anyone* can get X-rated video cassettes, and our children are getting them. One study indicates that the prime purchasers of pornographic materials are teenagers between the ages of twelve and seventeen.[26]

Pornography Opposes Reality

Fantasy is really what pornography is all about. One pornographer reported in an article in *Rolling Stone* magazine that "the future is assembly line sex, not actual [sex] . . . but fantasy."[27]

Miss Playmate of the Month sounds so friendly and outgoing. Her script is always the same. She tells you that she likes to ski, listen to music, travel, and read books—all the things you like to do. But most of all, she wants to do it—with you. She's so willing to bare her perfect breasts and make herself available to you. But in reality, if you asked her to show you her breasts she would probably call the police. So you must take them—after all, that's really what she wants you to do, and you're living in a fantasy.

Pornography is a lie. Few (if any) women want to have sex forced on them. Pornography is a lie because it can lead one to believe that he is actually having sex with someone when all he is really doing is masturbating. Pornography is a lie, because it leads one to believe that all the perverted things he sees—the whips, the multitude of partners, the bondage, the homosexual acts, the donkeys and the dogs, the anal sex—are normal. It is a lie because it leads one to believe that this is what sex is all about.

Pornography is a lie because it rejects the distinctions between the sexes and the complementarity for which males and females were created. It is a lie because it mocks God's created order for man and woman to become one flesh and to be fruitful for Him, and as such it must be rejected.

EIGHT

MASTURBATION

*P*erhaps no other form of sexual activity has been so soundly condemned and yet more universally practiced as masturbation.

Considered a device of the Devil during the Victorian era, there was no end to the list of its horrible effects on body, mind, and soul. No doubt the longest list was published by Dr. John Harvey Kellogg, the man who gave us Kellogg cereals. According to Kellogg, the consequences of sexual self-abuse included:

> . . . general debility, consumptive symptoms, premature and defective development, sudden changes in disposition, lassitude, sleeplessness, failure of mental capacity, fickleness, untrustworthiness, love of solitude, bashfulness, unnatural boldness, mock piety, a tendency to be easily frightened, confusions of ideas, an aversion to girls in boys, a distinct liking for boys in girls, round shoulders, weak backs, paralysis of the legs, an unnatural gait, bad sleeping positions, underdeveloped breasts in girls, capricious appetite, a fondness for irritating substances (salt, pepper, spices, vinegar, mustard, clay, plaster, slate pencils, and chalk), a disgust with simple foods, use of tobacco, paleness, acne, fingernail biting, shifty eyes, moist cold hands, heart palpitations, female hysteria, chlorosis ("green sickness"), epileptic fits, bed-wetting, and the use of obscenity.[1]

To be sure, Mr. Kellogg was not alone in his condemnation of masturbation. Scores of others, including the most respected medical authorities, had similar lists, which included such effects as blindness, insanity, and abnormal growth of bodily hair.

While the myths of the past have largely been dispelled, controversy still surrounds the practice of masturbation. Although fears concerning any physical danger resulting from this sexual practice have proven to be false, questions about the sinfulness and emotional effects of solo-sex continue to plague both the secular and Christian world. The range of opinion on this topic stretches from the belief that masturbation, though not a health problem, is immature, to the belief that masturbation is a positive part of our human sexuality.

The view that auto-stimulation is immature is most common among traditional psychoanalysts. The argument, according to researcher Carole Offir, is that although masturbation plays a crucial role in the development of sexuality during childhood and adolescence, it can be a sign of neurotic disturbance in adulthood because it prevents a person from developing "true genital heterosexuality" and because it functions as a substitute for sexual intercourse in a person who fears loss of ego if he or she enters into a relationship with another adult. The assumption is that a person who functioned satisfactorily in coitus would not want to masturbate.[2]

Less traditional psychoanalysts and many other mental health professionals suggest that health or neurosis depends on what the person feels and thinks during masturbation and why the person does it. Psychoanalyst Virginia Clower believes that in adult women masturbation can be either normal or pathological, depending on whether or not it reflects underlying emotional conflicts and infantile desires. However, for Clower, even "healthy" masturbation is at best a crutch when intercourse is either unavailable or inappropriate.[3]

Finally, a number of psychologists and sex therapists take the position that masturbation is not only harmless, but is actually a perfectly vaild way to get rid of sexual tension and is simply one alternative among many in the sexual repertoire of the human experience.[4]

Even Christians are divided in their opinions about masturbation. Thus one author writes:

> . . . masturbation is objectively a serious sin. Except in rare cases, it is also subjectively sinful, and the average person who

gives in to masturbation, either as a teenager or as an adult, commits sin.[5]

Herbert Miles, on the other hand, argues that masturbation can be sinful or not sinful depending on the situation. It is sinful when its sole motivation is sheer biological pleasure unrelated to anything else, or when it results from inferior feelings and causes guilt feelings, or when it is associated with sexual fantasy and lust. But it is not sinful if it is used without fantasy as a program for limited and temporary sexual self-control during the peak time of one's sexual drive until marriage.[6]

Still another Christian writer states that the practice of masturbation to release pent-up genital tension is not of itself a sin. Indeed, argues Joyce Huggett, tension-relieving masturbation "is not unlike scratching your head to relieve an itch, sneezing or stretching after a period of prolonged inactivity."[7]

Certainly such varying opinions can be confusing, especially to those who are often frustrated with feelings of guilt and shame as they struggle with the habit of masturbation in their own lives. Much of our confusion would surely disappear if the writers of Scripture had addressed the topic of masturbation, but the fact of the matter is that the Bible nowhere mentions the practice. Some Christians use the story of Onan who spilled his seed (semen) upon the ground as a proof-text to condemn masturbation (Gen. 38:8-10); but this passage clearly refers to *coitus interruptus* during sexual intercourse and not masturbation. The reason God was angry with Onan was because Onan used the practice of *coitus interruptus* as a means of disobeying the Levirate marriage law. The issue was not over the evil of masturbation, but over the evil of disobedience to the Word of God.

With the experts divided and the Scriptures silent, we might ask if there is really good reason to pursue the issue any further. If masturbation is a sin, it's surely one the Bible deals with less than gossip, envy, or jealousy. Perhaps in our eyes it is a bigger issue than it is in God's eyes.

Moreover, we must also realize that the Bible's silence on the specific topic of masturbation does not mean we are left on our own. However, be that as it may, thousands of people continue to struggle with it, many of whom feel perverted, guilty and full of shame. Therefore, I believe we must press on further in this area until we feel we have some basis of resolving the issue. Graciously, God has given us principles in His Word through which we can filter specific experiences. One thing is certain—God has not remained silent about our sexuality, nor is He silent about the nature of sin. He has told us what we must know about our sexuality and why He has created us as sexual beings.

God's purpose for sexual expression finds its ultimate fulfillment not in one's hand or through a vibrator, but in the context of a loving relationship between husband and wife. Sex was meant to be fruitful and as a means of deep communion between two people (Gen. 1—2). Moreover, God has set specific boundaries for sexual expression which when followed keep us spiritually, psychologically, and physically under God's protection both in our own lives and in our relationships with others (1 Thess. 4:3-8). Sin, on the other hand, always moves us away from God's design and purpose for our lives (Rom. 7:14ff.).

These are some principles which can help guide us through areas which are less clear. We should also remember that not every decision we make in the Christian life is between what is right and wrong. Some decisions are between what is good and what is best. Thus, we may avoid taking certain actions not because they are sinful, but simply because they are not profitable or best for our lives. Nor should we forget that even good things can become harmful if overindulged or taken to extremes.

Let's take another look at this area and see if there might be some principles that may help guide us in our understanding of masturbation.

The word *masturbation* comes from two Latin words: *manu* (meaning "hand") and *turbatio* (meaning "to disturb" or "agitate"), or possibly from *manu* and *stuprave* (meaning "to defile"). Masturbation is the self-stimulation of the sex organs, usually by hand or fingers, resulting in orgasm. Because the word *masturbation* has carried negative connotations over the years, many people prefer to use other words such as self-stimulation, auto-stimulation, auto-eroticism, self-manipulation, or solo-sex; but they all refer to the same activity.

Although no one really knows how many people practice masturbation on a regular basis, studies by Kinsey,[8] McCary,[9] and others show that almost all men have at times practiced masturbation—with the percentage of women being somewhat lower. Moreover, masturbation seems to be common at almost every age level.

Children sometimes masturbate as part of their physical self-exploration. They may discover that playing with their genitals brings a certain pleasure without fully understanding what they are doing. Parents who discover their children in the act of masturbation must be careful in how they react. Scolding or shaming young children for a natural discovery may cause the child to associate sexual pleasure with the idea that such pleasure is dirty or sinful. Such ideas can carry on into later years and marriage and may cause feelings of guilt or shame over the pleasures of sexual intercourse, which may cause problems in the marital relationship.

Adolescents also masturbate. As sexual feelings begin to intensify throughout the teenage years, many boys begin to use masturbation as a way to relieve sexual anxiety. Wet dreams or nocturnal emissions often help relieve this sexual tension, but many continue to use conscious masturbation for sheer pleasure. As a result, young people often feel guilty and become obsessed with a struggle against masturbation. Many Christian youth find themselves weeping and praying and making promises to God which they find they cannot keep. The guilt feelings are thus intensified, because they not only feel guilty about masturbating but also about not keeping their promise to God.

Many people continue to masturbate on into adulthood and even after marriage. One might ask why anyone who can experience sexual fulfillment in marriage would want to masturbate. There are a number of answers to this question. One reason is that there may be times during the course of marriage when sexual intercourse is not possible. The later stages of pregnancy and for a few weeks after the birth of a child are usually times when sexual intercourse is not possible. Military duty or business trips may also separate couples for prolonged periods of time during which a husband may imagine his wife alongside him as he stimulates himself or the wife may imagine her husband in the same way.

Other reasons married people masturbate, however, may reflect personal problems or problems within the relationship. Psychologist Clyde Narramore states that feelings of sexual inadequacy may underlie masturbation. People who do not have satisfactory heterosexual relationships may feel a need to prove that they are sexually adequate. Through masturbation they may consciously or unconsciously attempt to prove to themselves that they are capable of normal sexual functioning. Or a husband, for example, may never have achieved sufficient adjustment in his own personality development to allow him to have a normal relationship with his wife. He may practice masturbation as a way to avoid intimate sexual relations with his wife. On the other hand, some husbands may be well-adjusted, but their wives suffer from personality disorders and may not want to have normal sexual relations with their husbands. In the case of some couples, the wife may be an aggressive and domineering person with whom the husband feels threatened and uncomfortable. This, in turn, may cause him to practice masturbation.[10] There are, of course, chronic masturbaters who are given to their own erotomania fed by fantasy and pornographic material.

What emerges from what we have learned so far is that masturbation, although widely practiced, does not easily fit into any one particular pattern. It is practiced by males and females of different ages and for different reasons. Certainly the young boy who discovers the pleasurable feelings that result from self-stimulation is participating on a different level than the adult who practices masturbation on a regular basis to satisfy the lustful fantasies that arise from his addiction to pornography. So what shall we say? Is there a way to sort this all out and come to any firm conclusions about masturbation?

Since Scripture is silent on the particular topic of masturbation, we must be open to the possibility that hard and fast conclusions may not be possible. This does not mean, however, that we should automatically dismiss the possibility that masturbation may be detrimental to our well-being. We must consider whether or not this practice threatens to violate any other principles of God's Word. Thus, while firm conclusions may seem to elude us, the dangers which can accompany masturbation can be readily seen in light of other Biblical principles. I would like to emphasize that these principles do not speak directly to the issue of masturbation, but are guidelines to help us construct a position on the *dangers* of masturbation.

First, masturbation may be harmful to a person's well-being when it is associated with inappropriate sexual fantasies. Sex researcher A. C. Kinsey and his colleagues discovered that some 90 percent of all males who masturbated had used fantasies as a source of stimulation during masturbation.[11] This fact concerns us for two reasons. First, sexual fantasies usually follow prurient interests. Psychologist Carole Offir states:

> . . . fantasies rarely center on the kind of sex that is most strongly approved in our society—standard, missionary-style, heterosexual coitus with one's permanent partner. Instead, they typically involve some sort of forbidden behavior. A person may imagine sexual activity with an anonymous stranger, an acquaintance, or a famous person, like a movie star; sexual activity with more than one person at a time; a situation in which the person forces someone to have sex or is forced by someone; activity involving techniques that the person would not ordinarily use; or sex with someone of the same gender.[12]

Often these fantasies are fed by the use of pornographic materials which are designed to stimulate sexual excitation in people's minds. Such fantasies reduce people to sex objects and are clearly meant to appeal to selfish lust.

Jesus warned against such fantasies in Matthew 5:28—"anyone who looks at a woman lustfully has already committed adultery with her in his heart" (cf. Prov. 6:25; 2 Pet. 2:14). This is not to say that all thinking about sex is wrong or harmful. In fact, some thinking about sex is quite natural. People don't enter their wedding night without any idea of what is going to take place. It is natural to think about sex, and indeed, as we have already noted, it is even natural to dream about sex, dreams which sometimes result in nocturnal emissions. But these are not the kinds of behavior to which Jesus was referring.

What Jesus was condemning were those fantasies in which we see ourselves possessing that which we are not allowed to have. He is condemning those fantasies in which we manipulate people in our minds in ways that will appeal to and satisfy the lust of our imagination. Whether it be a forbidden partner or a forbidden sexual practice, we must be aware of the fact that the mind is capable of endless perversions. Paul's exhortation to the Philippians is certainly an appropriate word to the area of our fantasies as well: ". . . whatever is noble, whatever is right, whatever is pure, whatever is lovely, whatever is admirable—if anything is excellent or praiseworthy—think about such things" (Phil. 4:8).

I would suggest that the main reason many people who masturbate struggle with such terrible feelings of guilt is due to the context of their thought-life as much as anything else. The problem is that if fantasies occur during masturbation, the resulting pleasure is reinforcing and the fantasies tend to persist.

Another problem with sexual fantasies is that they usually have little to do with real life. Sex in the mind is colored with ideals—flawless partners, perfect in body and face, wanting nothing more than to satisfy sexual whims. Real people, of course, rarely meet the qualifications of a fantasy. What often happens is that the chronic fantasizer may find that his or her partner in "real" sex is less erotic than his fantasy, and he may therefore continue to fantasize during sexual intercourse about someone or something else. Such a situation is hardly the meeting of persons God intended sexual intercourse to be.

Second, masturbation may be detrimental to our well-being when we feel we have no control over it. Many people have discovered that masturbation can become compulsive and addictive, even to the point of becoming an obsession. As such, it is a bondage which can hold one tight in its grip. Surely this kind of bondage undermines the Scriptural injunctions to be self-controlled (cf. Gal. 5:23; 2 Pet. 1:6).

Ironically, however, masturbation has been recommended by some experts as a means of maintaining sexual self-control. Dr. Herbert Miles cautiously suggests that masturbation can be used as a kind of escape valve for the physical release of sex drive in males.

> We must teach that it is within the Christian understanding of God's plan and purpose for a young man's life that he may practice, without being sinful, *a limited, temporary program of masturbation* from the time he approaches a peak in his sexual drive until he is married . . . the emphasis here is *self-control* in order to avoid yielding to the temptations of immorality.[13]

But Miles' argument is weak. First, it compares the sex drive to something like a steam boiler which must let off built-up steam or explode. This view of sexuality probably accounts for the idea proposed by some that masturbation is easier to control if sexual energy is diffused by wearing yourself out playing sports or working hard. However, while strenuous activity may help take your mind off sex, there is not necessarily any transfer of sexual energy. Otherwise, athletes and hard-working laborers would have the least sexual energy of anybody. Evidence seems to indicate that physically active people have a stronger sexual libido than those who are less active.

Second, using masturbation as a means to lower your sex drive does not work. In fact, the opposite has been found to be true. The sex drive is better compared to an appetite—the more it is fed, the more it demands. The end result is that, rather than curb the sex drive, masturbation tends to stimulate it. Thus, masturbation may actually undermine self-control.

A third difficulty with masturbation is that it may move us away from God's intended design for sex. It is not simply another option one is free to choose from the repertoire of human sexuality, nor can it ever be equal to sexual intercourse between a man and a woman. At its very best, masturbation is second-rate sex which falls far short of the union the Creator purposed sex should be. Would anyone argue otherwise?

> One is free to do his own choosing when masturbation is an option.
> . . . if one is open to the possibility of masturbation and to the value of masturbation, then a sexual relationship with another person becomes a matter of choice rather than a matter of necessity. . . .
> . . . masturbation can be seen as the expression of an urge toward the independence of an individual from other people.[14]

Such statements obviously demonstrate either a gross misunderstanding or a total perversion of what sex is all about. Masturbation is completely separated from procreation and the intense communication which takes place when two people come together and meet in sexual intercourse. Masturbation is fruitless—it produces no children, no love for another person. Sex is meant to be shared, to be interpersonal; masturbation is selfish and intrapersonal and therefore directly opposed to what sex is meant to be.

121

To conclude that masturbation is wrong or sinful in every situation may be saying more than the Bible itself says; that does not mean, however, that we cannot come to any firm conclusions. We may, in fact, conclude that masturbation has the potential to be sinful or wrong when it involves the use of inappropriate fantasy, when it becomes obsessive, or when it is seen as another option for sexual intercourse.

Moreover, we may conclude that masturbation certainly is not *best* for our lives. As we noted earlier in the chapter, much of what we struggle with in the Christian life is not between what is right and wrong, but between what is good and best for our lives. If, then, masturbation is less than best, and if it has the potential of being detrimental to our spiritual and emotional well-being, it is probably better that we opt not to engage in the practice.

But how does one stop if one desires to break away from this habit? Anyone who has tried to quit knows how hard it is. While there have doubtless been many suggestions, no particular plan can guarantee one will stop. More depends upon the person than the plan. Nevertheless, allow me to suggest a few ideas which may assist those who wish to control their struggle with masturbation.

First, *stop!* That may sound oversimplistic, but that is where the process must start. It involves a conscious decision that one must make before the next temptation to masturbate arises. Often our problem is that we fail to make a clear, firm decision before a tempting situation arises; instead, we find ourselves trying to make up our minds in the throes and heat of the battle. When we find ourselves in a war between our mind and our genitals, the genitals will surely win most of the time *unless* we have made our decision beforehand.

"But I have stopped," you say, "at least a hundred times!" "You don't know how many times I've promised God never to do it again!" That may be a part of the problem. We often set our goals so unrealistically high that they become impossible to us; and because they're impossible, what's the point in trying to live up to them? Instead of vowing to *never* do it again, simply make up your mind to not do it today! Anyone can stop for one day. By taking it a day at a time, we set realistic goals and increase our likelihood of succeeding.

Second, *take control of your thought-life.* Certainly we cannot stop every thought from coming into our minds, but we can control what we do with it once it's there. We can either entertain it or send it back out. It's a conscious decision. And it takes discipline.

This does not mean that we are to pretend that inappropriate thoughts are not there, but simply that we choose not to give them expression. Paul admonishes us to "put to death, therefore, whatever belongs to your earthly nature: sexual immorality, impurity, lust, evil desires and greed, which is idolatry" (Col. 3:5). This has both a negative and positive aspect to it. Negatively, we are to avoid those things which might incite our lust and evil desires; and positively, we are to set our thoughts on whatever is true and right and pure (Phil. 4:8).

Third, *break patterns which might set up masturbatory practice.* We tend to be creatures of habit, even in our sexuality. Often we find ourselves doing things, even things we don't like, as a matter of routine. If you find that the greatest urge to masturbate, for example, is when you get into bed at night and you are alone with your thoughts, it may be helpful to do something to break up the routine. Try reading, writing letters, or even doing the crossword puzzle until you're tired enough to go to sleep. You might even find yourself getting smarter in the process!

Fourth, *avoid sexually stimulating material.* Pornographic magazines, books, and videos will definitely undermine your ability to maintain sexual self-control and maintain a pure thought-life. Steer clear of anything or any place that you know will bring you down. Furthermore, don't ever test whether or not you've overcome something by submitting yourself to it once again. Such testing is only playing with fire, and you will get burned.

Fifth, *don't concentrate on your guilt, but on your forgiveness.* Often we make the mistake in our Christian walk of focusing on the guilt in our lives rather than the forgiveness we have through Jesus Christ. We should not ignore guilt, but neither should we allow it to beat us into the ground until we feel that victory will never be ours. If you feel that masturbation is wrong and you slip, ask God to forgive you, thank Him, and go back to Step One. If you let it, guilt will keep you in bondage, sometimes to the point where you figure, "What's the use—I may as well give up trying." The Apostle John, writing to Christians, said: "If we confess our sins, he is faithful and just and will forgive us our sins and purify us from all unrighteousness" (1 John 1:9). Believe it, and move on to other areas of your life.

Sixth, *stop hating yourself.* Many people feel terrible about themselves after masturbating; some have even expressed disgust and hatred. People often feel that they are no good and that they will never make it. But such ideas are simply lies of the Devil. Remember that Satan is the accuser of the brethren (Rev. 12:10) and the father of lies; he will try to convince you that you are "no good" and that "you can't make it" in order to keep you from victory. But the truest thing about you isn't what Satan or anyone else says about you; it is what God says that counts, and God says He loves you (Rom. 5:8).

Seventh, *continue to cultivate your walk in the Spirit.* "But the fruit of the Spirit is love, joy, peace, patience, kindness, goodness, faithfulness, gentleness and self-control" (Gal. 5:22). Self-control is a product of the Holy Spirit living in the believer. Begin each day anew by submitting your spirit, mind, and body to the Lordship of Jesus Christ. Ask for His strength; He will surely give it.

THE LAST TABOOS

*P*eople who sneak around backyards of neighborhoods hoping to find someone undressing through the crack of a bedroom curtain, or get their sexual thrills by exposing their genitals to an unexpecting stranger, or dress in the clothes of the opposite sex, or get off by inflicting pain on others, or sexually molest children, or have sex with animals are not the things about which one should have to write, much less read. But neither are they the sort of things one can ignore, for they are the pitiful things which happen among the masses of humanity and sometimes among those we know and even in the families of our brothers and sisters at church.

Although some of their deeds occur more often than others, none of them fall into what could be considered as normal sexual behavior. Sometimes they are the result of wounded relationships that have cut so deep into a person's being they have completely restricted their mental or emotional growth. Sometimes they are the result of a reprobate mind carried to the most wicked extreme of unsatiated lust. But they all exhibit a bondage to sexual appetites which attempt to feed some desperate need in a person's life. And they all demonstrate that sex is capable of endless perversions when it is removed from the purpose for which God created it.

Technically known as *paraphilias* (from the Greek *para* meaning "beside, beyond or amiss" and *philia* meaning "love"), the behaviors mentioned in this chapter have one chief characteristic in common: they are abnormal and in most societies taboo. (Or at least they were. Have we forgotten our social scientist friends?)

For the social scientist, what is abnormal is ultimately a subjective judgment. They are not judgments based on moral absolutes, but made within a particular cultural and social context—and of course they change. Because abnormality is relative, some so-called "experts" on human sexuality have tried to abandon the concept entirely.

Sociologist John Gagnon, for example, takes a qualitative approach and focuses on the statistical incidences of a given sexual behavior in the general population. He calls those who practice unconventional sexual behaviors "sexual minorities" and implies that rarity is the only thing that sets off these behaviors from other sexual activities.[1]

Others use consent as a criterion for establishing abnormality. John Money of Johns-Hopkins University in Baltimore contends that pathology depends on whether the partner does or does not consent to the behavior.

> . . . bizarreness is not the issue. Thus if a man needs his partner to urinate on him in order to get an erection, this would be pathological only if the partner did not want to cooperate. The existence or absence of consent often determines whether a particular sexual behavior is regarded as a crime. It is perfectly legal for a man to gaze at a woman as she undresses if she permits him to do so; it is a crime if he spies on her through a window. Nudity is fine in the bedroom but is barred in public, where a passerby may view it unwillingly. The criterion of consent recognizes that the social context in which a behavior is performed influences judgments of abnormality.[2]

What is implied in these views is that what is normal is morally permissible. And since nothing is really considered abnormal, any type of sexual behavior is acceptable. This thinking, of course, is totally disconnected from a Biblical view of sexuality, as well as from a Biblical view of sin. To be sure, there is still a nearly universal consensus about some of these behaviors. No one, for example, would suggest that sexual attraction of a dead body (necrophylia) is normal. However, such a consensus is not made on philosophical grounds, but because it is personally nauseating to most people. But then so was oral-anal sex fifteen years ago.

The pornography industry has also done a great deal to make even the most bizarre sexual behavior seem normal. We have already noted in our chapter on pornography the growing number of magazines and films which are aimed at promoting particular sexual perversions ranging from bondage and transvestism to pedophilia and anal obsessions (there are nearly one hundred titles that deal specifically with the last perversion alone). Even the so-called soft porn magazines such as *Playboy* and *Penthouse* accept and promote such sick and perverted practices as sadomasochism, incest, and bestiality. While their promotion of such practices is certainly subtler, it may actually be more dangerous. With readership in the millions, the method these widely accepted magazines use is to depict these perverted practices in cartoons. By placing grossly abnormal sexual behavior in the context of "humor," people's attitudes toward them are subtly disarmed. Instead of recoiling from such behavior in anger and alarm, people find themselves laughing and thereby acknowledging that such perversity is nothing to be alarmed about.

But be alarmed we must. If society continues to deny the basis of any moral absolutes, and if present attitudes about sexual liberation, pornography, and homosexuality prevail, we will continue to see sexual behavior move toward more aberrant and bizarre expressions. We have already seen the progression of perversion in pornography move from showing women's breasts in the 1950s to sex with animals in our present time. This very same movement is being paralleled in the sexual practices of our own society. Rampant promiscuity, adultery, homosexuality, and transvestism are now accepted as part of our American culture, scarcely raising an eyebrow or causing a sigh of despair.

Despite the outcries of child abuse, new cases continue to mount up every year. Although accurate statistics simply aren't available, child sexual abuse is now recognized as far more prevalent than once imagined. According to records compiled by the American Humane Society, there were 7,559 reports of child sexual abuse in 1976. In 1983 annual reports escalated to 71,861, an increase of over 850 percent.[3]

Many believe that the problem only seems more prevalent because it is more openly discussed. However, it is not unreasonable to contend that the deterioration of the family structure and values, along with the unlimited boundaries of sexuality in today's society, including a three-billion-dollar child pornography industry, has contributed to an increase in child sexual abuse. One child molester with more than forty victims, many of whom were sons and daughters of friends, said, "I thought sex was a good thing, the more of it the better."[4]

While "flashers" may expose their private parts, they and other sex offenders are strongly disinclined to reveal their private sex lives. Obviously most are not willing to risk discovery by coming forward for interviews, and those who are caught and jailed typically conceal the full nature and extent of their sexual offenses for fear of new charges and lessened opportunity of parole.

Nevertheless, a recent study of outpatient sex offenders conducted by psychiatrist Gene Abel and psychologist Judith Becker discovered some disturbing information which suggests that various types of deviant sexual behavior are common to the typical sex offender, and that the number of deviant sex acts committed by the average offender is far greater than had generally been supposed.

For example, among 159 men who admitted to incestual offenses with girls and women, a number of additional offenses were also reported:

> Forty-nine percent had molested young girls and 12 percent young boys outside the home; 6 percent were frotteurs (rubbing against people); 7 percent were voyeurs (peeking at people); 20 percent were exhibitionists; 19 percent were rapists of female adults; and 12 percent had committed homosexual incest at home.[5]

Moreover, the number of deviant sex acts committed by the average offender in the research sample was far greater than anticipated, with the average individual committing 520 deviant sex acts during a twelve-year period.[6]

The study also revealed differences in the ages at which various types of sexually deviant arousal began. For more than half, voyeurism began before age fifteen, homosexual sex with children before age sixteen, frottage before age seventeen, and exhibitionism before age eighteen. Most of the studied offenders had developed aberrant sexual interests and fantasies by the ages of twelve or thirteen before committing any sex acts. Abel and Becker concluded, on the basis of their patients' self-reports, that deviant sexual behavior, which begins with deviant sexual fantasies, develops when the fantasies become linked with masturbation and are "rewarded" through orgasm.[7] This is the same process we saw take place in homosexual development and again demonstrates the power of sexual fantasy when it is associated with masturbation.

But why some people act on their fantasies and others do not, and what triggers more bizarre or perverted fantasies in some than in others is still not clear. However, when one begins to realize the connection between sex and the mind, a better picture begins to emerge. It is the mind or the imagination which really helps keep a person's sexuality alive. The mind is quite capable of imagining very graphic pictures of sexual experiences. So powerful are these pictures that they can actually cause physiological changes such as increased heartbeat or penile erection.

But the mind along with its ability to create powerful sexual images also has the ability to pervert and distort those images. Often when sexual fantasies become obsessive, especially as they are reinforced with masturbation, new variations must be imagined or inserted into the fantasy in order to keep a high level of sexual excitation. This can eventually lead to the person imagining the most bizarre and perverted sexual experiences.[8] This might also explain why many people who are sexual deviants engage in numerous sexually perverted behaviors.

However, others may become fixated at one particular place in their sexuality or find themselves sexually aroused over one particular object. A young boy, for example, who is sexually aroused by women's underwear and reinforces that sexual excitation through masturbation may become so fixated on women's panties that he is not able to achieve sexual arousal except through presence or thoughts of women's underwear. Such a fixation is called a fetish, which we will look at later in this chapter.

At any rate, whether one progresses toward more sexually bizarre behavior or becomes fixated on a particular object or experience, almost all sexual perversions have a *compulsive* quality— that is, the person finds it impossible to resist performing the act.[9]

We should also probably note that most of the sexual behavior we are about to discuss not only invariably becomes obsessive, but is more common in men than in women. This may be because men tend to be more sexually stimulated by what they see or by what they can imagine than women are. Many sexual perversions involve little if any actual sexual contact with another person and tend to be more visually oriented instead. Although sexual stimulation and excitation is usually present, sexual contact is often avoided at all cost.

Another reason I believe men tend to be more inclined toward sexual paraphilia, again, has to do with the sexual distinctions between the sexes and the way sexual identity unfolds. As I suggested in an earlier chapter, a woman's sexuality, unlike that of the man's, unfolds naturally as part of the rhythm of life. She does not need to *discover* her sexuality because her body is continually telling her and reminding her of what her sexual destiny will be. The development of her breasts and her monthly period, for example, remind her of her potential to be a mother. It is difficult to ignore these obvious reminders, and therefore it is more difficult for a female to become "fixated" on some particular sexual behavior which takes her away from what her sexuality was designed for.

Men, on the hand, have no such reminders. A man has a penis, but it is hardly given to the natural rhythms of life. Its sexual repertoire is limited to one thing—ejaculation, an event which is largely regulated by man's choice. It certainly is not a natural cycle constantly reminding him and calling him back to purposeful sexuality; as a result, male sexuality has, to a greater degree than female sexuality, the capability of becoming "fixated" at a certain point or on a certain object (e.g., women's underwear). With nothing reminding him to move on, he may, for various psychological or emotional reasons, remain fixed at one place in his sexuality, while still maintaining certain sexual gratification, albeit through some bizarre or perverted behavior.

Sigmund Freud distinguished two general types of paraphilia which are accepted by most psychiatrists and psychologists today: in one type, the choice of sexual object or partner is unusual; in the other, the act itself is unusual. Fetishism (sexual attraction to an inanimate object) is an example of the former type, while exhibitionism (exposing one's genitals in public) is an example of the latter.

Beyond these two general descriptions, I wrestle with how far we should go in explaining or describing the pitiful depths to which man can sink in his sickness or the tragic extent to which he can carry his twisted lusts. To pursue it much further runs the risk of doing so simply for the sake of our own curious titillation.

At the same time, we cannot afford to close our eyes or bury our heads in the sand. As we are about to see, sexual perversion knows no bounds. It is capable of such wicked degradation it staggers the imagination; and for those who are held in bondage by sexual sin, help is desperately needed. But if the church ignores the fact that these destructive practices exist, we will be limiting our ability to respond to these needs in any purposeful way.

I believe that the task of the church is to function as both a prophetic and reconciliatory community.

First, it must stand prophetically in a secular culture and declare without compromise "thus saith the Lord." The prophetic ministry of the church is to warn us of what happens when we stray from or choose to ignore God's commands and purposes for our lives. The Word of God and secular culture do not share the same perspective on the nature of man and how he ought to live, especially in regard to man's sexuality. Nor is secular society silent in expressing its views. There are persuasive voices in our culture which are shaping the attitudes of men and women, young people, and children alike in regard to their sexuality. Perhaps one of the loudest in this area is the voice of relativism—it is heard at almost every level of society.

Thus, at the academic and clinical level, for example, we have people like Dr. John Gagnon, professor at the State University of New York, who, as we saw earlier, has suggested that we banish the concept of abnormal sexual behavior altogether. Why? Because abnormality is relative. Rather than defining sexual deviancy in terms of sin or even psychological sickness, he prefers to define such behavior in terms of their statistical occurrence, implying that the only thing we can use to discriminate normal sexual behavior from other kinds of sexual activities is frequency. Moreover, since those who practice "unconventional" sexual behavior are in the minority, what is needed is not help, but better equal rights protection.

At the popular level, we are told that it is not our business if homosexuals and lesbians teach our children in public schools and that whatever two consenting adults want to do in the privacy of their own homes is up to them. But sexual deviation is no longer a topic of concern but of national curiosity. Television and radio talk shows fill the airwaves with special guests who readily talk about their particular perversion and how persecuted they are and how they wish people understood them.

Such programming is seldom given a Biblical point of view or even a neutral one. On a recent local television program in San Diego three transvestites, their wives, and two psychotherapists from the University of California, San Diego, were the special guests. When, toward the end of the program, the question was asked, "Is there anything wrong with men dressing like women?" one transvestite responded with, "How could there be—God made me this way!" To which one of the psychotherapists added:

> The only thing wrong with cross-dressing is society's unacceptance of it. But there is nothing wrong with it.[10]

He obviously did not know or perhaps wasn't concerned with Deuteronomy 22:5.

Sex therapist Dr. Ruth Westheimer, whose advice column on sex appears in newspapers all over America and who also has a popular TV show, is another example of popular sex propaganda which undermines a Biblical understanding of sex. In a recent column a woman wrote inquiring what she should do about her husband's addiction to pornography. Dr. Ruth's advice? She suggested that the woman leave her husband alone since such behavior was quite normal *and that she see a psychotherapist to find out why pornography bothered her so!* In other words, the husband didn't have a problem with pornography—she did![11]

And, of course, the evolution of rock and roll music has always maintained its front-running pace in pushing lyrical content to the furthest extremes of sexual perversion. From Dr. Hook's "Freaker's Ball" which describes a pervert convention including references to homosexuality, leather fetishes, sadomasochism, and incest; to Alice Cooper's "I Love the Dead," an anthem to necrophylia (sexual attracation to dead bodies): "I love the dead before they're cold/the bluing flesh for me to hold"; to Prince, whose third album received the following review from *Rolling Stone* magazine:

> Nothing could have prepared us for the liberating lewdness of *Dirty Mind*. . . . The cover photograph depicts our hero, smartly attired in a trench coat and black bikini briefs, staring soberly into the camera. The major tunes are paeans to bisex-

uality, incest and cunnilingual technique. . . . at its best *Dirty Mind* is positively filthy. Sex, with its lasting urges and temporary satisfaction, holds a fascination that drives the singer to extremes of ribald fantasy.[12]

All of this suggests that the world is very confused indeed about sexual behavior. But such confusion is quite predictable in a society that refuses to acknowledge any Biblical absolutes. The church has an opportunity to shine God's light on human sexuality to a sexually confused world, but it must be prepared to speak to the issues, as difficult or perverse as they may be. If not, the relativistic morals of this world will lead us into greater bondage than we've ever known.

The second task of the church is to live as a community of love, acceptance, and reconciliation. The message we proclaim is not just that we are sinners who are broken, hurt, and in need of restoration (although until we've heard the bad news about ourselves we can never hear the good news of the gospel), but the message of the gospel is that God loves sinners! He came to heal and bind up the bruised and broken. He came to save the lost.

I believe some of the most wounded and broken people in our society are those who are bound to the power of sexual perversion. But I also believe that the power of Jesus Christ can break the chains that bind these people and set them free. Healing and restoration can only take place, however, in an environment conducive to change.

It takes great courage and a great sense of desperation for those who are caught in sexual sin to come forward and seek help. The church must be prepared not only to forgive, but to help such people work through their problem. I will speak more directly to this in our next chapter, but it's important for us to realize that we are up against giants. And while the power of God is more than adequate to slay every giant of sexual perversion, it might do us well to briefly survey the land which holds so many captive.

We can accomplish this purpose without going into great detail except to briefly describe the behavior and to show how such behavior is destructive to God's design for the sexes. Some perversions are obviously more common than others, although even some of the more rare practices are receiving more publicity and therefore acceptance through the means of pornography.

Voyeurism

A voyeur (from the French word *voir,* "to see") is a person who seeks sexual arousal by secretly observing others undress or engage in sexual activity. Another term for a voyeur is *peeping tom.* According to English legend, during the eleventh century the husband of Lady Godiva promised to lift a burdensome tax on his tenants if his wife would ride naked through the town of Coventry on a white horse. Lady Godiva accepted the challenge, and in deference to her bravery all the townspeople agreed to stay indoors—all except Tom the Tailor, who peeped at her and promptly went blind. Virtually all voyeurs who are caught or reported are, like Tom, male.

Voyeurism can be seen in minor forms in those individuals who view and read pornographic material and who frequent topless bars and burlesque theaters. However, voyeurism is not normally associated with this kind of looking. What sets voyeurism apart from this kind of viewing is that a voyeur prefers looking over any other sexual activity and prefers to watch someone who is unaware that she is being observed.[13] The behavior is usually compulsive, and the voyeur may spend many "unproductive" hours looking or waiting in great discomfort and at great risk in order to have a chance to peep.

In fact, risk may be part of the compulsion in voyeuristic activity which adds to his excitement. Most voyeurs show little interest in nudist camps or the kind of socially permitted opportunities for sexual looking such as topless bars.

Voyeurism most frequently occurs among young single men, but it is also found among older and married men. In the latter case the individual usually exhibits an inadequate sexual adjustment in marriage.

One of the basic dynamics underlying voyeuristic behavior may be a serious feeling of inadequacy in the sex role. Often the voyeur may have difficulty establishing healthy relationships with the opposite sex. Fearing actual sexual contact, he resorts to viewing the opposite sex for gratification instead. This enables him to avoid the associated fears of sexual involvement.

Another factor which may underlie this behavior is lack of sexual understanding and an immature attitude toward sexual activity. Sometimes a child who grew up without adequate sexual understanding may develop a deep curiosity about human sexuality. Feeling that sexual matters are taboo, he turns to "peeping" as an attempt to satisfy his craving for sexual knowledge and stimulation.[14]

EXHIBITIONISM

Exhibitionism is a sexual deviation in which an individual feels compelled to expose his sex organs in an inappropriate situation in order to gain sexual excitement. Again, most exhibitionists ("flashers") are men. The exhibitionist usually displays his genitals (and sometimes masturbates) in public places such as parks or schools and frequently to children of the opposite sex.

Often exhibitionism seems to involve more than just a desire to gain sexual arousal or gratification; a need to shock the viewer or express contempt and hostility also may accompany indecent exposure. Sometimes exhibitionists prefer victims of a certain age or social class, as one man candidly revealed:

> Middle-aged women, smartly dressed, no one else. Someone who reminds me of my mother, a doctor said once, he pointed that out to me, and I think he might be right, that I'm still trying to insult her. No, it's not a prelude to a sexual assault, there's never anything like that in my mind. Just to shock. If a woman looks disgusted and turns away, then I'm satisfied. A woman smiled at me once and came towards me instead; I ran away from her as hard as I could. . . .
>
> I can't tell you why I do it; when it's happening I'm not conscious of anything except this feeling of being contemptuous towards women and wanting to try and give one a shock.[15]

The basic personality pattern underlying the behavior of the exhibitionist is usually that of inadequacy, insecurity, and low self-esteem. A man who has inadequate feelings in his role as a male may have a compulsion to demonstrate his masculinity by publicly displaying his genitals. By shocking someone through this display, the exhibitionist gains a feeling of power and sexual virility.

Another possible explanation for exhibitionism is hostility toward the opposite sex or society at large. Exposing may be a way of expressing contempt and anger in much the same way some people turn their hostility toward society through crime or other antisocial acts.

It is important to note as we go how little the people who are involved in these practices actually engage in any intimate, loving, physical contact with the opposite sex.

FETISHISM

Fetishism is a term applied to someone who gains sexual arousal through contact or attraction to a particular part of the body or some inanimate object. The body part may be sexual, such as the breasts, or it may be nonsexual, such as the feet. The inanimate object is most often an article of clothing, such as underwear or shoes. Again, fetishists are nearly always male.

It is, of course, fairly normal for many people to be somewhat aroused at the sight of certain features of the body (such as large breasts, or shapely legs) or by certain articles of clothing (such as lacy bras or underwear). Such a response does not make a person a fetishist. What characterizes true fetishism is a compulsive attachment to the fetish and usually the inability to achieve sexual arousal or gratification without it.[15]

As in the case of exhibitionism and voyeurism, one of the dynamics underlying fetishism is a strong feeling of inadequacy in relation to members of the opposite sex. He may be unsure of his sexual role and refuses to become sexually involved with someone for fear of rejection or humiliation. Or, for the person who is afraid of emotional intimacy, the fetish may put emotional distance between the person and his partner.

In addition, some behaviorists explain fetishism as a result of accidental conditioning in which during earlier development sexual gratification was associated with some object or article of clothing. Having received sexual arousal from one experience, combined with fear of actual sexual contact with the opposite sex, the individual may develop a consistent pattern of sexual gratification through inanimate objects. Offir cites the case of a man who developed a fetish for plaster casts.

> At age eleven he broke his leg. An attractive nurse held his bare leg so that the cast could be set, stimulating his thigh and producing an erection. Later he masturbated while thinking about the incident. Eventually he amassed a collection of actual

136

casts to use during masturbation and heterosexual intercourse.[17]

TRANSVESTISM

A transvestite is a person who wears the clothing of the opposite sex, usually for the purpose of his own sexual arousal. Some
individuals wear only undergarments of the opposite sex, while
others may dress entirely in such apparel. Transvestites are nearly
always male and are for the most part heterosexual. In a survey of
subscribers to a magazine called *Transvestia,* 89 percent of the
respondents considered themselves heterosexual, and over three-
fourths were either married or divorced.[18]

The dynamics of transvestism are similar to those found in
fetishism, except that instead of using one article of clothing for
sexual arousal, the transvestite uses a whole costume, and he actually wears the clothing. How the transvestite uses cross-dressing to
achieve sexual arousal depends upon the individual. He might masturbate while observing himself in a mirror, cross-dress in public
and attempt to pass as the opposite sex, or masturbate to memories
or fantasies of public excursions. This behavior is indicative of an
inability to accept one's sexual role.

SADISM

A sadist is a person who receives pleasure from inflicting pain
or abuse on others. While sadism can occur in any kind of relationship, our concern here is with those who must inflict physical pain
or humiliation in order to achieve sexual gratification. The terms
sadist or sadism are derived from the name of the Marquis de Sade
(1740-1814), a French novelist and soldier who wrote about such
brutal exploits as hanging women from the ceiling and whipping
them as his servant manually stimulated his genitals. The Marquis
was eventually admitted to an insane asylum.

Psychologist Clyde Narramore suggests that sadistic behavior
may be related to several factors. In some cases it may reflect
generalized feelings of hostility. By inflicting pain upon a sexual
partner, the sadist may feel that he has gained a sense of power and
superiority or has repaid society for its misdeeds to him. In other
instances sadism may be an expression of rage and hostility toward
the sadist's mother. Some men may attempt to ventilate angry and

137

resentful feelings toward their mothers by inflicting pain or abuse on their partner during sexual intercourse. Again, men who feel inadequate and insecure in the masculine role may turn to sadistic behavior in order to prove their masculinity.[19]

MASOCHISM

Masochism is the converse of sadism. Instead of hurting or abusing others for sexual gratification, masochists inflict pain on themselves either by their own actions or by inviting others to hurt or abuse them. Moreover, their sexual aberration is found more frequently among women than men. One reason which may account for this is that males usually tend to be more aggressive, while females tend to be more submissive.

More severe forms of masochism include bondage (being tied up), discipline (being whipped or spanked), and subjecting one's self to beating, choking, spitting, and verbal abuse. Masochistic males sometimes visit prostitutes who specialize in sadistic acts. The prostitute and her client may engage in elaborate role-playing, in which she plays the part of the mistress and the client the part of the slave. Individuals who lead lives that are governed by great self-control or responsibility have been known to engage in this kind of behavior.[20]

Some have suggested that underlying masochistic behavior is a felt need for punishment. For example, a person who has grown up with the idea that sex is sinful or dirty may feel a conscious or unconscious need for punishment for participating in sexual activity later on. By submitting to serious pain, a woman may attempt to "atone for her sinfulness."[21] Such behavior, of course, is based on seriously distorted sexual attitudes.

PEDOPHILIA

A pedophiliac is a person who attempts to gain sexual gratification through sexual activities with children. It may include either heterosexual or homosexual experiences. The child is almost always forced into the heinous activity, although the adult often will convice the child that sexual behavior between adults and children is a good thing to do. It must be emphasized that his perversion is the fault and responsibility of the adult and not the child.

The pedophiliac is a pitiful person who has failed to develop mature adult heterosexuality. Insecure in his role as a man, he may feel threatened by the possibility of engaging in sexual intercourse with adult women. Often such people show a tendency to relate inadequately with adults at any social level. Fearing adult sexual involvement, the pedophiliac directs his sexual drives toward children where his fear of being proven sexually inadequate or inferior is lessened.

RARE PARAPHILIAS

In addition to the sexual perversions already discussed, some people engage in a variety of more degrading sexual activities. Many of these practices usually considered extremely rare are now more familiar, especially through increased attention given in pornographic material, some of which caters to and specializes in many of these perversions.

Bestiality, or zoophilia, is sexual intercourse with animals and may include masturbation of an animal or the performance of oral sex on an animal.

Frottage is the practice of obtaining sexual arousal by rubbing one's genitals against an object. In its most common form, a man rubs his genitals against a fully clothed woman, usually in crowded public situations, such as on a bus or subway. It may go unnoticed by the woman.

Urophilia is sexual stimulation from an interest in urine. Also known as "golden showers," the urophiliac may gain sexual arousal by watching others urinate, urinating on others, being urinated on, or even drinking urine.

Corpophilia is sexual arousal gained from excrement and involves the same sorts of activities that urophilia does.

Necrophilia is sexual interest in corpses. The necrophiliac may be aroused simply by viewing the corpse or by actually having intercourse with it. Necrophiliacs are usually psychotic.[22]

The list could go on, but we have said enough already. The sobering truth is that man's wicked imagination knows no bounds. The reprobate mind is capable of losing all sense of morality, purpose, normality, and reality. It is capable of taking God's wonderful purpose and design for human sexuality and perverting it beyond recognition.

Without exception, the perversions of this chapter fail to meet God's design and purpose for the sexes and their relationship to one another.

Perhaps the most obvious thing lacking in these sexual aberrations is the authentic meeting of persons in meaningful sexual intercourse. It is a sure sign of emotional or psychological trouble when sexual activity takes place with no concern for intimacy with another person of the opposite sex. Sex becomes an isolated, depersonalized, and lonely act of desperation. Peeping through windows, focusing on inanimate objects, and turning to animals for sexual gratification miserably and tragically avoids the greatest opportunity to engage in the joys of committed sexual intimacy.

Nor do the sexual behaviors we have mentioned in this chapter give opportunity to freely participate in our God-given privilege of procreation, either symbolically or in actuality. Instead, it is sexual stimulation turned inward, performed compulsively and devoid of the love and care two people can share together.

As we have seen, so many of those who are bound by these perversions of God's glorious design for men and women feel worthless, inadequate, guilty and hopeless. One might wonder if there is any possible way of breaking free from the bondage and recovering once again God's gift of true sexuality. The answer, of course, is absolutely yes!

God by His mercy, power and grace can rebuild the ruins of shattered sexuality, as we shall see in our next chapter.

PART III

RETURN TO BIBLICAL SEXUALITY

REBUILDING THE RUINS

*I*t's June and another beautiful, sunny day here in Southern California. Looking at the palms and neatly planted flowers growing beyond the back patio, it seems a little out of place that as I sit here prepared to bring this book to a close, my thoughts should turn toward Christmas. But there has been a carol humming through my mind all morning—"Joy to the World." In particular, it is the third verse of this great song by Isaac Watts that won't let go of my thoughts.

> No more let sins and sorrows grow,
> Nor thorns infest the ground;
> He comes to make his blessings flow
> Far as the curse is found,
> Far as the curse is found,
> Far as, far as the curse is found.

In the past few pages of this book, we have seen just how far the curse is found. The curse, with its sins and sorrows, grows deep within the nature of every man (and woman) and overflows into every aspect of his being, wreaking destruction and ruin wherever it can.

It is found in the physical realm, invading our health with sickness, sometimes twisting our bodies with disease, and always hastening our way toward death. It is also found in the depth of our emotions, taking advantage of hurts and offenses in order to harden our hearts and sever our relationships. So it is not surprising that we should find the curse assaulting our very sexuality and with it the image of God it reflects.

To be sure, the nature of sin always destroys or distorts the image of God to some degree. It is the business of the Tempter to see to this. In fact, he is compared in Scripture to a roaring lion who prowls about looking for someone to destroy (1 Pet. 5:8). It is, in a certain sense, his only way of fighting against God. Satan learned in his unsuccessful revolt against God that he has no power to bring his attack directly against God Himself; instead he must channel his destructive activity toward the next best thing—the image of God in man. Because man's sexuality as male and female is so bound to the image of God and the purposes of God in this world, it is targeted for special assault.

Thus if the image of God is found in the polarity of the sexes as male and female, what better way to destroy the image than by persuading man to exchange his sexual distinctiveness for androgynous masks? Or if the purposes of God are accomplished through the unique contribution of each sex working together to build strong families, what better way to sabotage them than by fostering so much dissatisfaction with one's sexual role in life that she is willing to abandon marriage, children and heterosexuality in the name of equal rights? Or if sexual intercourse itself is purposeful and meaningful in being fruitful for God through procreation and in establishing the meeting of persons in the bond of mutual commitment, what better way to undermine purpose and meaning than by convincing us that sex can be equally fulfilling as an egocentric and anonymous recreation? Why not depersonalize sex through the means of one's own hand, fantasizing over pages of a magazine, peeping through bedroom windows, or any other means which keep people from meeting face to face? In the end the growth of sins and sorrows destroys not only the distinction between sexes, but sex itself.

But the power of the curse is not unbreakable! It does not extend so far that it can't be reached by the love of God. Our carol has good news—"He comes to make his blessings flow far as the curse is found." From the deepest sorrow of the homosexual to the most perverted compulsion of the paraphiliac, the power of God through Jesus Christ is not only able to break the bondage of sexual sin, but to heal the hurts and wounds that lie beneath the surface of sexual behavior and to restore sexual wholeness again.

This chapter is about opening our lives to the flow of God's blessings. It is about letting God wash away the debris and wreckage of shattered sexuality and allowing Him to rebuild the ruins of broken men and women.

And it is a rebuilding process. No sin is easy to overcome, especially those indulged in to the point of compulsion. The more entrenched the compulsion is, the harder it will be to overcome. Even so, there is no sin or habit that is so strong that it cannot be broken by the power of God. Nor must any habitual sin lock us into an inevitable destiny over which we have no control. Nevertheless, I believe there are certain things which must happen if we are to break free from the power of sexual sin. In the remainder of this chapter we will explore the process of rebuilding sexual wholeness.

A Desire to Change

No one can change without a desire to do so. That desire is essential in overcoming any habit or obsession, sexual or otherwise. Moreover, the desire to change must come from the person himself. A desire on the part of someone else will not do—it must be a person's own choosing.

For example, a husband may attempt to change some aspect of his life in order to please his wife. But often his attempts are only made as concessions to her. He may be motivated by his wife's deep desire that he change, but because *he* has not yet seen the need in his own life the results are usually short-lived. Until he desires the change, most attempts to reform will be futile.

But what causes a person to want to change? Doesn't the fact that a person continues to do something indicate that he really enjoys what he's doing? The answer is no. Sexual obsessions are usually rooted in behavior which causes not only intense sexual arousal, but intense feelings of guilt and shame as well. A person may even make promises with himself or with God that he will never do a certain activity again, but then find himself breaking those promises time and time again. Thus, a person may find himself continually doing something he knows he shouldn't do or does not even want to do. Why is this?

First, we must realize that sexual arousal is a very powerful force by and of itself. However, in addition to the intense emotional and physical rush experienced as part of normal sexual excitement, many people with sexual obsessions find sexual arousal in an atmosphere of risk and danger. Psychologist Earl Wilson states:

> Although emotion is still not fully understood by psychologists and physiologists, it is clear that emotion involves both physiological components such as hormonal secretions and cognitive components such as labeling the internal experience. For example, a person may look across the street and see the neighbors undressing for bed. Since many people believe that spying on their neighbors is wrong, violating this value may result in an aroused state. A feeling of danger may precede any feelings of arousal. The person may be saying, "I shouldn't look!" But if the person looks anyway, he or she may become aware of bodily sensations. As the couple undresses, the watcher may interpret those bodily sensations as sexual arousal. It may be impossible to say which came first, the fear arousal or the sexual arousal. In fact, the two sources of arousal may have combined to create an unusually high state of arousal.[1]

In other words, the deviancy itself may be a stimulating factor. "Many men report that they are stimulated by women at topless bars and in X-rated movies, not because of their exceptional beauty but because they aren't supposed to go see them."[2] As a result, the intense feelings which come from the deviancy itself may incorrectly be labeled as sexual excitement. Thus, a person may come to think that the deviant behavior is needed for sexual arousal, and we have the making of an obsession.

According to Wilson, obsessions are developed when a thought that results from any form of sensory stimulation is pursued—that is, when the person follows it up so it can happen again. For example, "if the original stimulus is visual, pursuit involves taking another look. If it is physical, pursuit involves touching again or seeking to be touched." Each time a thought is pursued, it becomes stronger and involves more aspects of the person. Pursuit of the thought leads to the development of a belief such as "I must experience this" or "I have to have this at all costs." This belief about the thought leads to the formation of a filter which ensures that all future experience is interpreted from the perspective of the belief. Filters negate certain negative features of the behavior such as the possibilities of being caught or the consequences of being discovered, while accentuating the positive aspects such as the sexual stimulation of the experience.[3]

One aspect of the filtering process is what Wilson calls *labeling*.

When my behavior gives me positive feelings, I may begin to label myself in terms of that behavior. For example, if I enjoy a few concerts I may label myself a music lover. If I do not like the concerts I may say I'm not musical. The interesting thing is that the label controls my subsequent behavior. If someone asks me to a concert I may say yes because I have labeled myself a music lover, not because I like the group that is playing. Labels we give ourselves related to sexual obsessions may be similar. Labels like "I can't control it," "I'm always horny" and "I have strong needs" are common. These labels result from previous positive feelings, and they also support our continuing involvement in the obsession.[4]

Filters may also be used to include or exclude certain sexual behaviors. Homosexuals, for example, usually have a filter which says, "I am not aroused by persons of the opposite sex." Some people have developed filters that say they are only aroused by children or certain articles of clothing, or viewing certain kinds of pornography, or other deviant kinds of behavior. One of the strong objections to pornography is that is can cause people to develop filters that are socially or Biblically disapproved. On the positive side, we may also develop filters which prevent us from being aroused by children or members of the same sex. Many men have shared the experience of being aroused by the slender figure and long blonde hair of someone walking down the street, only to have the person turn and reveal a full beard! Suddenly they are no longer aroused because their filter says, "I am not sexually aroused by members of the same sex."

The next step in the development of a sexual obsession is that actions are generated by the belief. The person who believes that he must have pornographic material to achieve sexual satisfaction will find ways to view it (even if he must do so secretively). As he views more and more pornography, both the belief and the filter are reinforced. In fact, the person may continue to act on his thoughts even though the material excites him less, simply because his beliefs and filters are so strong. In turn, the beliefs and filters grow stronger as they are acted upon until the person finds himself caught in a self-perpetuating cycle of obsessions.[5] This whole process helps explain why many people with sexual obsessions *feel* like they are out of control or can't stop. It also explains why men will risk their jobs, their reputations, and even their marriage and families for a peek through a neighbor's window or an opportunity to make sexual advances to children.

Ultimately, however, no one can deny his own personal responsibility for his sexual obsession. While it might appear that such a self-perpetuating trap might make it difficult, if not impossible, for anyone to break away from it, the truth of the matter is that it is not impossible. What it will take, though, is an admission on the part of the perpetrator to admit that his behavior is wrong and that the cycle of obsession must be broken. But the desire to quit must be greater than the desire to continue on. At some point the person must be able to detach himself from his behavior and come to honest confrontation with himself and see his need to change.

What are the things that enable a person to see his need to change? I believe there are three main things that may encourage a person that there is a better way and inspire a desire to change.

The first is *conscience*. Conscience can be explained as the innate agent which bears witness to my behavior in light of my moral value system. When my behavior violates my moral value system, the conscience creates psychic pain we call guilt.[6] When sex is enjoyed through the means provided by God in Scripture, it is accompanied by a sense of peace and harmony, pleasure and satisfaction, and a little bit of awe and wonder. And unless I have been taught that sex is dirty or wrong (part of my moral value system), my conscience is quiescent—it has no need to condemn my behavior because that behavior has not violated my moral value system, which in this case has been informed by the Word of God. However, if my sexual activity violates my moral value system (set by God and/or society), I will experience guilt which may be accompanied by feelings of shame, emptiness, worthlessness, and fear.

To be sure, the conscience can be unreliable if it is not trained properly or if it is continually ignored. People often feel guilty about certain things, not because they have anything to do with morality, but because they thought they did. That is why it is important to train our conscience with the Word of God. But even if one is not familiar with God's Word, there is a morality innate within man that, when it is violated, causes guilt and pain (Rom. 1:18ff.). This probably explains why certain practices such as incest are nearly universal taboos.

Thus, with the witness of God's Word written on both the pages of Scripture and the human heart, and the witness of societal laws and taboos (which really are based on God's Word), it should not surprise us that most of those who are sexually deviant experience tremendous feelings of guilt. Sometimes the guilt, combined with feelings of loneliness, emptiness and despair, becomes so intense that a person may feel there is no way of escape. I believe these feelings account for the abnormally higher suicide and alcoholism rates among those with sexual obsessions, particularly homosexuals. Yet, at the same time it may be these same feelings which cause a person to say, "I've had enough—I need help!" Just as physical pain tells us something is wrong with our bodies and motivates us to seek help, so can psychic pain motivate us in the same way.

The second thing which may bring about a desire to change in a person is *truth*. Unless a person is willing to confront the truth about his life, he will never see the need to change. In fact, the reason someone falls into sexual obsession in the first place is because somewhere along the line he has suppressed the truth (Rom. 1:18, 25). And yet, there are those who have been trapped in sexual obsessions who have been set free who at some point have confronted the truth again and instead of rejecting it have believed it. When the Holy Spirit (who is the Spirit of Truth) convicts us of sin and error, he also convinces us of the truth (John 16:8-13). It is truth, Jesus said, that ultimately sets us free (John 8:32).

The third thing which may cause a person to want to change is *fear*. The fear of getting caught, the fear of getting AIDS, or the fear of losing one's family may not necessarily by itself be enough to cause someone to want to change and break away from their sexual obsession. As we have already seen, risk and danger sometimes contribute to the obsession. But if that fear is realized or comes close to being realized, it can sometimes have a way of jolting a person to his senses. A minister recently confessed that it was not until he had been arrested for exhibitionism and had to face his congregation with the news that he realized just how far his sexual obsession had gone.

But whatever it takes—whether it be guilt, a confrontation

with truth, or finally getting caught—there must come a point in the person's life when, if he is going to be set free from the grip of his obsession, he desires to change more than anything else. Only then is he in a position to begin rebuilding the ruins.

DEALING WITH THE PROBLEMS OF SIN

I believe that all the perversions of Biblical sexuality are sin. Whether we think that homosexuality or transvestism or peeping through bedroom windows for sexual arousal is harmless or not is beside the issue (although it can certainly be argued that these are not harmless activities). What is at issue is that such practices violate the principles of Scripture and are therefore offensive to Almighty God. They undermine and distort His design and purpose for sexuality, and in doing so mock the image of God in man.

I also believe that we can't deny personal responsibility for our sin. There are those, of course, who would argue that they were born with a certain sexual inclination or that they can't help doing what they do, and therefore it cannot be considered sin. Such ideas, however, are not true.

But there is another level at which sexual deviancy may be sin which goes beyond the particular act or behavior. It has to do with how one responds to the events or people which gave cause for the deviancy to develop.

Often sexual deviancy is rooted in childhood. We have already seen that traumatic experiences such as incest or rape or the withdrawal of a father's love and affection can set a response pattern that may give rise to aberrant sexual behavior. For example, the young boy who is sexually molested by another male may have developed a sense of sexual arousal in the context of a same-sex experience which may carry on into later life. Or the young boy who is berated by his father for not being able to do something that is particularly "manly" (e.g., play football) and is told that he is a "sissy" and should "go play with the girls" may take up an affinity with his mother. If he overidentifies with the female role, he may move toward homosexuality. Certainly these are circumstances which lie beyond the control of the child. In a sense the child who has been sinned upon may end up perpetuating the offense in another way. But while we cannot be responsible for the actions of others, we must take responsibility for our response to them.

How then should we respond to the offenses of others? First, by forgiving those who have offended us. This may be difficult, but it is essential for restoring personal wholeness and for receiving our own forgiveness. Jesus said:

> For if you forgive men when they sin against you, your heavenly Father will also forgive you. But if you do not forgive men their sins, your Father will not forgive your sins. (Matt. 6:14, 15).

Unforgiveness, then, blocks not only our relationships on the horizontal level, but the vertical level as well. Thus, the resourceful healing power of God we need for wholeness in our own lives is undermined by our refusal to forgive others.

The second way we must respond to the offenses of others is by accepting the fact that our reaction-response to these offenses has contributed to our condition. We cannot blame genetics or insist that there is nothing we can do. If through the help of a skillful counselor we are able to see how our response to past circumstances or relationships has influenced our present behavior, we must now be willing to change that response. Even though that offense may have occured many years ago, people often continue to carry feelings of hatred and anger through the years. These feelings may be harbored at an unconscious level but can nevertheless reinforce present behavior. If we refuse to confront our sin at the deeper levels of offense, we may be guilty not only of the sinful act itself, but also of refusing to confront the larger issues of our sins and allowing them to control us. In essence, what we are saying is that we don't wish to resolve the problem.

But once we have admitted responsibility for our sin, we open the door for forgiveness and repentance. We must be willing to accept forgiveness. First, we must accept the forgiveness of God. The Bible is very clear that "if we confess our sins, he is faithful and just and will forgive us our sins and purify us from *all* unrighteousness" (1 John 1:9). There is no sexual sin that God will not forgive. Nor will He hold sin against us—"as far as the east is from the west, so far has he removed our transgressions from us" (Psa. 103:12).

Second, we must be willing to forgive ourselves. The Bible tells us that Satan is an accuser (Rev. 12:10). He would like us to believe that because we really don't deserve to be forgiven, we therefore ought to continue to feel guilty about our past sins. He would like us to believe that our sins were so deplorable that we really can't be completely forgiven. But the Bible also tells us that Satan is a liar. We are not forgiven because we *feel* forgiven, but because God has declared us forgiven (1 John 1:9).

Forgiveness is important, but so is repentance. Repentance really means two things. First, it means *stop!* Stop and turn away from your sin. Stop the direction you're going. Stop wandering the neighborhood looking for cracks in the shades! Stop going to the X-rated movies! Stop driving in that part of town! Stop doing whatever you're doing that's bringing you down! "But I can't stop!" Yes, you can. And if you can stop just once, you can stop twice, and if you stop twice, you can stop three times. Instead of stopping forever—just stop once.

Stopping, however, is not enough. You must do an about-face. You must turn and go in a new direction. The Apostle Paul exhorts us:

> Do not offer the parts of your body to sin, as instruments of wickedness, but rather offer yourselves to God, as those who have been brought from death to life; and offer the parts of your body to him as instruments of righteousness. (Rom. 6:13)

I have discovered that when this advice is taken literally, it has proved to be tremendously helpful for people with various problems. Strange as it may sound, I have suggested that people actually make a formal, verbal dedication of their "unruly" body parts to the Lord. If gossip is the problem, I have recommended specifically dedicating the tongue to God. I have urged young people to specifically dedicate their genitals to the Lord. I tell them, before you go out on a date, tell your genitals exactly who they belong to! This is always met with a few chuckles, but there is something about verbalizing the agreement to yourself that gives it strength. One university student told me, "I never would have made it last night, but I remembered my agreement—it worked!"

REBUILDING A BIBLICAL PERSPECTIVE OF SEXUALITY

We live in a society that is saturated with sexual enticements and perversions of every kind. One of the questions I am most frequently asked by teenagers and young adults is, "How do I keep myself pure?" Interestingly enough, well over two thousand years ago someone else asked the identical question! In Psalm 119:9 the writer asks, "How can a young man keep his way pure?" And in the same verse he gives us the answer—"By living according to your word."

One of the most common problems among the thousands of men and women who involve themselves in sexually deviant behavior is that they have never really understood their sexuality from a Biblical point of view. It is not unusual, for example, to find that many women involved in practices such as masochism were also raised with the idea that sex is dirty, wrong or sinful. Caught in a dilemma between the pleasures of sex and the idea that it is wrong, a woman may find herself submitting to masochistic practices, using the pain and abuse as a way of alleviating the guilt of sexual enjoyment.

Part of the healing process is understanding the nature of our sexuality. There are three important truths that all men and women should understand about their sexuality if they are going to live in personal wholeness.

The first truth we must understand is that we were created as sexual beings, differentiated as male and female—"male and female he created them" (Gen. 1:27). There are those in our society, such as the feminists, who would have us believe that our distinctions as male and female are not important. Instead, they prefer that we ignore such distinctions in favor of emphasizing the "true humanity of all persons without regard to sex." But there is no such thing as ascending to some "true humanity" which transcends sexual distinctions, because in the end humanity is ultimately made up of individuals who are either male or female. It is the first and foremost distinction by which we are known. From the moment we are born we are identified in terms of our sexuality. The doctor never exclaims to the mother who anxiously asks about her baby, "It's a person of true humanity!" or even "It's a baby!" We already know these things. What we want to know is how will this baby live out its purpose and function in life—"Is it a boy or a girl?"

The importance of maintaining our sexual differentiation has been covered in our first two chapters. Nevertheless, we should be reminded that in our sexual polarity we bear the image of God. Even as God is in fellowship with Himself, so we share in like fellowship as male and female. Personhood itself is experienced intrinsically as sexual orientation in terms of male and female.[7] And as we will note, it is through our sexuality that God accomplishes His purposes in the world. Therefore, the denial of one's own sexual orientation as either male or female, or the anonymity of sexual encounter outside the bond of a male/female relationship (e.g., sexual activity which denies the meeting of persons such as using pornography, voyeurism, exhibitionism, etc.) violates the divine order of our sexuality.

The second thing we must understand about our sexuality is that sex is good. God created us as sexual beings, with sexual urges and feelings; therefore, sex is not wrong, dirty or sinful. Sex is not only good, but it is extremely pleasurable (perhaps to insure that we would enjoy it often?). But the Creator also made sex to be purposeful and meaningful, and so He established guidelines to make sure that sex would remain so. It is when we deny the purpose and meaning of sex that it becomes sinful.

The third thing we should understand is that sex is purposeful. God created man as male and female and immediately gave them their first command—that they should be fruitful and multiply and fill the earth (Gen. 1:28). In issuing this command God was insuring that His creation would continue on. The primary purpose of sex is procreation.

Doubtless this idea does not go over well in a society which is falsely preoccupied with overpopulation and seeking personal pleasure. Even in Christian circles procreative sex is downplayed in favor of the benefits that result from sexual intercourse, such as pleasure and intimacy. While I would be the very last to deny that pleasure and intimacy are very important aspects of the sexual experience, I believe that we must be careful of allowing our orientation toward pleasure to supersede the fact that the natural consequence of our sexual activity (children) is what enables us to fulfill the divine command and insures that the pleasure God receives from creation is carried on.

This is why I believe sexual intercourse is confined to the permanent bond of marriage. If sex is supposed to produce children at least some of the time or even symbolically reflect our willingness to have them (not everyone can have children), then it is necessary to provide an environment of love and nurture and training for them. That is what families are all about, and that is what society is all about. Therefore, any sexual activity that is not reflective of a permanent bonding and meeting of persons and which does not reflect God's purpose for sex should be rejected. Thus, homosexuality, lesbianism, and many of the paraphilia mentioned in our last chapter must be rejected because, among other reasons, they fail to reflect even symbolically the procreative purpose of sex. Voyeurism, exhibitionism, bestiality, and the like must be rejected because, among other reasons, there is no meeting and bonding of persons.

One last thing we should note in this section—*marriage does not legitimize every sexual act even if both partners consent to it.* More than once I have heard Christians say that you can do anything you want in bed as long as you are married. They use the King James translation of Hebrews 13:4 which says that "the marriage bed is undefiled" as a proof-text, understanding it to mean that any sexual activity two married people agree to is condoned by the marriage. It is often used to justify the use of pornography, mild forms of sadomasochism, or oral-anal sex. But that is not what the writer of Hebrews had in mind. In fact, quite the opposite is true, and more modern translations make this clear.

> Marriage should be honored by all, and the marriage bed kept pure, for God will judge the adulterer and all the sexually immoral. (Heb. 13:4)

Again, sexual practices which deny the meeting of persons (we are not just talking about the meeting of bodies—it is possible to have sexual anonymity even between husbands and wives) or deny even the symbolic possibility of procreation (anal intercourse cannot produce children) must be rejected, even within the confines of marriage. Please do not conclude from this that I am suggesting that sex must be limited to one position with the lights out. Not at all! Sex is exciting, erotic, and creative, but it is not without limitations.

LEARNING TO OVERCOME TEMPTATION

Overcoming sexual sin is not unlike overcoming any other sin in the respect that success often depends on how well we are able to deal with temptation. In a very real sense, our struggle with sin will never be over until we meet our Lord face to face. So it is important between now and then that we learn how to fight our battles with temptation, for by His grace and power we can be overcomers. Allow me then to close this chapter with eight suggestions for dealing with temptation.

Realize That Temptation Is Inevitable

Being tempted is not something we can escape. Even Jesus, though He never sinned, was tempted (Heb. 4:15). We can learn to overcome temptations, but we cannot stop from being tempted. In James 1:13 the author writes: "When tempted," not "if tempted" and so assumes that temptation will surely come our way. Knowing that fact can work to our advantage. Cervantes said that to be forewarned is to be forearmed. Satan certainly knows our weakness, and he will do everything he can to get us to fall back into old sinful lifestyles. Knowing that he is on the prowl should keep us on our toes (2 Cor. 2:11; 1 Pet. 5:8).

Make Sure You're Starting with a Clean House

I once counseled with a young man who was addicted to pornography. After some time of seeing little progress in his struggle, I began to question him about matters we had covered earlier. "Have you thrown out all your tapes and books and magazines?" I asked. "Yes, I have," he said. "All of it?" I countered, emphasizing the all. "Well . . . I have kept one issue. . . ." Eventually I learned that he had been keeping one particular magazine at his office "just in case." He learned that it too had to go. And when he did, real progress started in his life. You cannot keep part of an addiction.

Don't Go It Alone

The battle is too big to fight by yourself. That is why the Bible instructs us to carry each other's burdens (Gal. 6:2). Sharing your struggle with a counselor or with a friend can be tremendously liberating for several reasons. First, sharing our struggle with someone we trust holds us accountable. When my actions are voluntarily made known to someone who will care about my struggle, and I give them permission to "check up" on me, I place myself in a position to be lovingly confronted with my sin. For example, if my struggle is with going to topless bars and I have made myself accountable to a pastor, counselor or friend who will be asking me from week to week how my struggle is going, the next time I am tempted to visit a topless bar I will either have to confess my failure to my friend or lie about my activity, neither of which I want to do.

Second, by sharing my struggle with a friend or counselor, I gain the opportunity of receiving new and helpful insight into my problem. I cannot always see the problems and patterns of my life as objectively as someone else might. The insight of others can be invaluable.

And third, I have the benefit of knowing that someone else cares for me and will be praying for me and encouraging me along the way.

Focus on the Source of Power—Jesus

There are no eight or ten or twelve easy steps to overcoming anything. They might be helpful, but ultimately it is our relationship with Jesus Christ that will change us and alter us. He is our source in a time of need. The writer of Hebrews says it best:

> Therefore, since we have a great high priest who has gone through the heavens, Jesus the Son of God, let us hold firmly to the faith we profess. For we do not have a high priest who is unable to sympathize with our weakness, but we have one who has been tempted in every way, just as we are— yet was without sin. Let us then approach the throne of grace with confidence, so that we may receive mercy and find grace to help us in our time of need. (Heb. 4:14-16).

Keep Spiritually Fit

Ultimately we must realize that our battle is not a sexual battle at all—at least in the physical sense. Our physical sexuality is simply the arena in which the real battle is being fought. Paul tells us that "our struggle is not against flesh and blood, but against the rulers, against the authorities, against the powers of this dark world and against the spiritual forces of evil in heavenly realms." Spiritual warfare at this level requires us to be spiritually fit. Two important exercises are essential for successful warfare—prayer and obedience to God's Word.

Prayer doesn't change circumstances and events as much as it changes and alters the one who is praying. I certainly believe that God can change circumstances—He could even remove the source of temptation—but often God uses prayer to conform us to His will, and in doing so He empowers us to do His will. The problem in temptation is that our will is contrary to the will of the Father; if it weren't, there would be no temptation. When in the garden Jesus was faced with the agony of the cross, He experienced a will that was different from the Father's, but he overcame it through prayer. "Take this cup from me. Yet not what I will, but what you will" (Mark 14:36). God can empower us through prayer if we submit our wills to Him.

Obedience to the Word is essential for overcoming sin. The psalmist who told us that a young man can keep his way pure by living according to the Word of God went on to tell us how: "I have hidden your word in my heart that I might not sin against you" (Psalm 119:11). It is not enough to know what God's Word says, but it must be internalized into the very fabric of our heart and mind. We must memorize it and meditate on it until it begins to transform the very way we think. As it does, we will discover that our actions will begin to align themselves with God's will for our lives.

Learn to Control Your Thought-Life

Sexual arousal gains its strongest impetus in the mind. In fact, the mind is easily our most powerful sexual organ. What we think about what we are doing or are about to do can play as big a role in our sexual excitation as what we actually do. Moreover, it is our thoughts that give rise to our actions. So if we dwell on some activity in our minds, those thoughts have the ability to arouse us and motivate us to act upon them. Jesus said it was from within, out of men's hearts, that sexual immorality, lewdness, and adultery begin and find their way into behavior (Mark 7:14).

If, then, we are what we think, it is extremely important that we learn to think right thoughts. Paul said, "We take captive every thought to make it obedient to Christ" (2 Cor. 10:5). How? Here are four suggestions:

(1) *Never feed lustful thoughts*. Thoughts have a way of generating momentum once we start them. Often the thought process starts with a particular cue that triggers a sequence of other thoughts. The cue may be something direct like pornographic material or indirect such as the memory of a past sexual experience. If we fail to avoid these cues or pursue them in any way, we start a

process that will soon have us living out entire fantasies in our minds. Obviously you cannot always stop certain images from entering your mind, but you can control them from that point. You can feed them or take them captive.

(2) *Objectify your situation.* One of the amazing processes of the human mind is that it allows us to step outside of our situation and surmise what is happening. You do have the ability to stop and tell yourself what's going on. And usually you do. Most people know where certain thought sequences will lead if they allow the process to continue. Often, however, we put up denial mechanisms in our mind; we'll pretend that we don't know what's going on, even though we really do. It is possible, however, to see the thought process unfolding before it actually does. At that point we must stop and visualize ourselves taking control.

(3) *Never reward improper thoughts with masturbation.* I have counseled with those who have tried to use masturbation as a way of controlling their thought-life. The rationale is that if you give the thought what it wants (sexual gratification) it will go away and that in the end this is much better than actually doing what was being thought about. The problem with this, however, is that reward will simply reinforce the thought, making it harder to control than before. You can't feed sexual fantasies and hope they'll go away—they must be starved.

(4) *Fill the mind with positive thoughts.* Pray without ceasing. The continual worship and praise of the Lord will make us increasingly aware of His presence in our lives. It's rather difficult to praise God and fantasize about sexual encounters at the same time. Again, the Apostle Paul exhorts us to fill our minds with "whatever is true, whatever is noble, whatever is right, whatever is pure, whatever is lovely, whatever is admirable—if anything is excellent or praiseworthy—think about such things" (Phil. 4:8).

Avoid Dangerous Situations

If pornographic movies are your downfall, stay away from that section of town. If your place for meeting men for homosexual encounters was in the park, stay out of the park. Don't cruise the red light district if it's going to be a temptation. This all seems so obvious, but it needs to be said. Don't test how strong you are by visiting old habitats—it's foolish.

Sometimes, however, we can't avoid certain places or people.

Or sometimes the people will come to you. Then what? The Bible tells us, "God is faithful; he will not let you be tempted beyond what you can bear. But when you are tempted, he will also provide a way out so that you can stand up under it" (1 Cor. 10:13). The key here is taking the way out that God provides. If you can't find it, turn around and start running—literally. Run until you're too tired to run back! Silly advice? I know many a man who wishes he had done something so silly.

Never Give Up

You may fall again before you overcome your particular sexual sin. You may think, What's the use? But you must never give up! C. S. Lewis once wrote:

> I know about the despair of overcoming chronic temptation. It is not serious, provided self-offended petulance, annoyance at breaking records, impatience, etc. don't get the upper hand. No amount of falls will really undo us if we keep on picking ourselves up each time. We shall be v[ery] muddy and tattered children by the time we reach home. But the bathrooms are all ready, the towels put out, and the clean clothes in the airing cupboard. The only fatal thing is to lose one's temper and give it up. It is when we notice the dirt that God is most present in us; it is the v[ery] sign of his presence.[8]

If you experience failure in your struggle with sexual temptation, you need to know it is not the end. The Apostle John, writing to Christians who, like you and I, were fighting to overcome the world, encourages us about the faithfulness of God: "If we confess our sins, he is faithful and just and will forgive us our sins and purify us from all unrighteousness" (I John 1:9).

You may lose some battles along the way, but don't lose the war. Never give up.

ELEVEN

REBUILDING THE RUINS IN SOCIETY

"*C*ivilizations are not murdered," observed historian Arnold Toynbee, "they commit suicide." Writing on the cause of the breakdowns of civilization, Toynbee was compelled to conclude with the poet George Meridith that ultimately "We are betrayed by what is false within."[1]

Indeed, throughout the history of our own nation we have been warned—from our Founding Fathers to the historians of our present century—that the greatest threat to America would not come from without, but from within. History has shown, moreover, that one of the marks of a society in decline has been an increased tolerance of and participation in sexual perversion.[2] Such was the case of ancient Rome—the ancestor of the Western world—and the same appears to be true of our nation today.

To say that we live in a society that is growing more sexually decadent is merely to state the obvious. Masturbation is promoted before a national television audience (via Phil Donahue) as the panacea to overpopulation, dull marriages, and safe sex.[3] Thousands of homosexuals march on our nation's capital to *demand* that the government find a cure for AIDS, but refuse to acknowledge any responsibility between the spread of this disease and their promiscuous lifestyles. After all, "AIDS is not a moral issue," Ron Reagan assures us (again over national television). "You don't get AIDS because you do bad things," the President's son tells us. "You get AIDS because you're unlucky."[4]

The continual growth and increasing perversion of the pornography industry provides a graphic illustration of our descent into moral decay. Forget the "hard-core" pornography offered in the adult bookstores (which outnumber McDonald's restaurants in the country by a margin of three to one); consider the "socially acceptable" pornography being sold over the counters of our supermarkets, newsstands, and convenience stores in our cities and neighborhoods. And what is "socially acceptable"? A full-length cartoon in *Playboy* shows an adolescent girl adjusting her skirt as she looks up at a man in his bathrobe, smoking his "after" cigarette, and exclaims, "You call that being molested?" (The idea is that children like being sexually molested.) *Hustler* offers a monthly cartoon called "Chester the Molester" depicting an adult male named Chester enjoying the abuse and molestation of children.[5]

The rise in child abuse, abortion, rape, and teen pregnancy makes it clear that our society is on the verge of committing sexual suicide.

What may be less obvious, however, is the way in which our nation is being morally undermined by an elite minority who are using their power and influence to shape the opinions and values of the larger population. Perhaps the most powerful of the elite is the news and entertainment industry. According to the A. C. Nielsen Company, 97 percent of the households in America own one or more televisions, and the average TV household uses the set more than forty-five hours per week.[6]

Despite the advent of cable and satellite networks, ABC, NBC, and CBS continue to be the principal source for news and entertainment for the majority of Americans. Moreover, a survey of television executives published in *Public Opinion* revealed that 97 percent of the television elite supported abortion-on-demand, 80 percent stated that homosexuality was not wrong, and a majority declared that adultery was not wrong.[7] Thus it is not surprising that what we have witnessed in these sources of entertainment (along with the movie and music industry as well) is a progressive abandonment of traditional Judeo-Christian values. Instead, we see the advocacy of a worldview which denigrates religion, marriage, and traditional sex roles and promotes feminist ideology, pre- and extramarital sex, abortion, homosexuality, and the validity of divorce. The media present this agenda of perversion as if it represents the consensus of American values, whereas in reality it does not. Nevertheless, by presenting it as the consensus, the media become a powerful means of persuasion and help to bring about a revolution in values. This campaign of values tranformation is furthered by the media's depiction of all who hold traditional values as unsophisticated, homophobic, or fanatical.

Also undermining traditional Judeo-Christian views of human sexuality is our public education system. The contemporary sex education offered in many of our nation's schools is imparting more than biological information about sex. From the first through the twelfth grade, schools are implementing a progressive curriculum of sex-education material designed to indoctrinate our children with aggressive feminist themes, desensitize them to homosexuality and other kinds of perverted sexual expression, and encourage them to explore their sexuality through masturbation.[8]

Textbooks used for social studies, science, health, and psychology are imbued with ideas and opinions stated as fact designed to sabotage basic traditional values. The following are examples of biased, secular values promoted in our children's textbooks:

". . . Everyone must develop his own set of principles to govern his own sexual behavior." (High School Psychology—*Psychology for Living*, McGraw-Hill/Webster Div., 1971, p. 182)

"The place, the opportunity, and their bodies all say 'Go!' How far this couple goes must be their own decision." (Grades 7-12 Sex Education—*Masculinity and Femininity*, Houghton-Mifflin, 1976, p. 21)

"Each instructor uses 'sex terms' differently. Write down all the terms referring to body parts and elimination and pronounce them in private, a little louder than necessary, or at a volume suited to the classroom." (Teacher's Discussion Guide, High School Homemaking—*Married Life*, Bennett, 1976, p. 8)

"Adolescent petting is an important opportunity to learn about sexual responses and to gratify sexual and emotional desires without a more serious commitment." (Grades 9-10 Health—*Life and Health*, Random House, 1980, p. 16)

"Contrary to past belief, masturbation is completely harmless and in fact can be quite useful in training oneself to respond sexually. . . ." (Grades 9-10 Health—*Life and Health*, Random House, 1980, p. 142)

"A person with variant sexual interests is not necessarily bad, sick, or mentally ill. . . . Rarely is any physical harm done to the child by child molesters and exhibitionists. . . ." (Grades 6-12 Homemaking—*Finding My Way,* Bennett, 1979, p. 218, 234)

". . . Divorce is considered an acceptable way of solving a problem." (Grades 6-8 Homemaking—*Homemaking Skills for Everyday Living,* Goodheart-Wilcox, 1981, p. 107)

Meanwhile, condoms and other means of birth control are dispensed through school-based sex clinics, and Planned Parenthood offers pro-abortion pregnancy counseling with referrals to local abortion clinics. Yet, despite a proliferation of information and increased state and federal expenditures on birth control and sex education, the rate of teen pregnancies and abortions continues to climb.[9]

Finally, even the elite powers of our own government have turned away from their responsibility to protect our nation from destroying itself. Politicians and judges are giving in to the increasing demands of the homosexual lobby to give homosexuals even *greater* rights than those afforded the rest of society. The failure of government to provide or enact legislation that would halt the spread of AIDS or to pursue dealing with this disease with the same caution afforded to other potentially dangerous communicable diseases reveals a bias which favors the libido of a homosexual minority more than the rights of the majority of Americans.

The 1973 Supreme Court decision in *Roe v. Wade* opened the floodgate of abortion-on-demand. There is still no federal legislation that would prohibit the sale and distribution of pornography, even though it has been shown that there is a *causal* relationship between exposure to sexually violent material and aggressive behavior toward women and that across-the-counter pornography promotes the sexual abuse of children (see Chapter 7). State and federal funding of abortion, public sex education, and feminist and homosexual organizations suggest that through our tax dollars we are supporting a system which encourages sexual permissiveness and perversion and tears at the foundation of society.

Although the number of people involved in the media and entertainment industry, public education, and the government is small in comparison to the rest of society, they nevertheless retain a profound influence in shaping the attitudes, values, and beliefs of the American public. Unfortunately, instead of using their resources to reinforce the values and traditions that would build strong families and a strong society, many of the participants in this elite group have used their influence to call into question or outright reject a Biblical or traditional view of sexuality.

Have they had an impact on our culture? *U.S. News and World Report* reported in December 1985 that there is a definite transition occurring in the prevailing attitudes toward sexuality in our country. The report, based on a poll conducted by the Roper Organization, segregated responses to questions about morality by age groupings to illustrate the shifts in moral perceptions along ten- and fifteen-year increments. Among other things, the poll revealed that while 60 percent of those sixty or older thought premarital sex was wrong, 78 percent of those eighteen to twenty-nine said premarital sex was not wrong. And whereas only 25 percent of those sixty or older said they would vote for a homosexual for President, 52 percent of the eighteen to twenty-nine-year-olds surveyed said they would vote for a homosexual President.[10]

Even in the Bible belt of the South—the bastion of Protestant, fundmentalist Christianity—traditional morality is falling fast. Louisiana State University sociologist Robert Soileau says, "If the Bible belt exists, it exists as a subculture. It's something to which people give lip service but which is not ruling their lives." John Sullivan, a Baptist pastor in Shreveport, Louisiana, adds, "[T]here has been a shift in ways of thinking about morality. We are seeing a decline in the moral climate in the Bible belt."[11]

The conclusion of all this would indicate that we are being influenced by a secular way of thinking and a set of values far different than the kind our Judeo-Christian heritage brought to us when sex was reserved for men and women in the commitment of marriage. As we saw in Chapter 2, at the core of this secular thinking is a rejection of God and the authority of His Word. Moral relativism has replaced moral absolutes and opened boundaries of our sexuality far beyond what God purposed them to be. The result has been sexual chaos. We are the victims of a sexual subversion based on godless thinking. The truth of Dostoyevski's words come back to remind us that "if God does not exist, everything is permitted."

The question which remains before us now is this: Can anything be done? Is there anything we can do to rebuild the ruins of sexuality in our society? I believe the answer is yes, but the reconstruction process will be costly in terms of time and personal commitment. How will it happen?

Cultural renewal begins with the individual. Since societies are made up of individual citizens, the character of a society is ultimately determined by the character, values, beliefs, and actions of individual citizens. Since cultural change results first from a change in the way people think and then the way in which they live, how we think at the individual level is of the utmost importance.

Moreover, how man thinks about and responds to the issues with which he is confronted, including his sexuality, will be informed by his personal worldview. By a worldview I mean the framework of philosophical presuppositions through which all of life is interpreted, including our sexuality. Included in our worldview would be our belief in or denial of the existence of God; our understanding of the origin and nature of the world; our understanding of the nature and significance of man; and our understanding of the origin and authoritative nature of morals and ethics.[12]

A Christian worldview believes not only that God exists, but that He has revealed Himself through His Word and His Son Jesus Christ; that the heavens and the earth were created by God and exist in an orderly and harmonious fashion; that man was created in the image of God and that his existence is meaningful and purposeful; and that truth is objective and knowable and contained in the authoritative absolutes of God's Word.

A secular worldview which denies the existence of God holds to the belief that the world was created by chance; that man himself is a product of chance and therefore without ultimate purpose or meaning; and that moral absolutes are unknowable or do not exist.

Not surprisingly each of these worldviews will ultimately bring man to a different conclusion about the expression of his sexuality. For the Christian, man's sexuality is informed by the fact that he is created in the image of God; it receives its purpose from the command of God in Genesis 1:28 to be fruitful and multiply, and is protected through the institution of marriage (Gen. 2:23, 24). The sexual order thus becomes the foundation of the family and consequently the social order.

Sexuality for the secular man, however, is not informed by any ultimate purpose, since man himself exists only as a product of chance. Therefore, sexuality is not bound by any absolute restraints. The sexual order is thus open to experimentation, resulting in the detriment of both the family and society.

It has been the testimony of history that the closer a society adheres to a Biblical worldview, the less it is beset by social upheaval and moral decay.[13] As Christians we realize that the only way this can happen with any lasting significance is through repentance and submission to the Lordship of Christ. However, one need not be a Christian to see the benefits of adhering to a Biblical view of human sexuality, both to oneself and society as a whole. But as author Barrett Mosbacker points out:

> A secular society cannot be expected to significantly conform its laws and mores to the Christian ethic unless that ethic is being clearly articulated, its benefits for the community and the individual explained, and more significantly its virtues modeled by the church.[14]

Therefore, if the Christian worldview is going to have any significant impact on the culture in which we live, we will have to address three challenges that presently threaten our ability to speak to the sexually decadent culture of our day.

The first challenge is to articulate for ourselves a thoroughgoing Biblical philosophy of human sexuality which would embrace the nature of man, the purpose of sex, and its connection to marriage and society as a whole. While much of this has been explained in greater detail in Part One of this book, a general outline for such a philosophy would include an understanding of the following components:

(1) Man was made in the image of God. We observed in Chapter 1 that God exists as a complementarity of fellowship. Thus man discovers that his own existence depends upon the complementarity of his sexuality. He is differentiated as male and female, each sex needing the other to fulfill God's purpose for their lives—to make the earth fruitful for God, a task accomplished through procreation.

(2) A primary purpose for sex is to produce children. Certainly there are other attendant benefits which result from sexual intercourse (the encounter of personhood, for example); but if unimpeded, the result will consistently produce children. This is not to say that every occasion of sexual intercourse will or even should produce children, but neither can we say that children are a mere accidental side effect of sexual intercourse.

(3) Marriage is a divinely appointed institution for producing and nurturing children. The complementarity of roles between the husband and wife are the primary means of nurturing children into the social order and into the Kingdom of God.

(4) The well-being and future of society depends on the sexual order described above.

Understanding this framework will, of course, have important implications for the individual, family, and society. Further, it will help us understand that God's commands concerning our sexuality are not arbitrary, nor were they simply social conveniences applicable only for the time in which they were given. Such a framework, among other things, allows us to define the perimeters of our sexuality. Many Christians today cannot articulate why they believe premarital sex, homosexuality, pornography, or other sexual perversions (many not even mentioned in the Bible) are wrong, other than to say, "Because they seem wrong" or, "Because the Bible says so." The fact that the Bible says so is true, but why does the Bible say so, and what do we say about those practices to which the Bible does not speak? When we understand God's purpose for sex, we are able to discern the rightness or wrongness of a sexual act by judging it against God's design and purpose for our sexuality. Thus we know that such practices as homosexuality, anal sex, or bestiality are wrong because they fail to meet God's design that sex be at least potentially or symbolically procreative and/or because they prevent a true meeting of persons.

Such a framework also reinforces the importance of marriage and sex roles in an age where both are being questioned and rejected at every level of society. Christians will have an easier time adhering to marriage and sex roles if they can see that they fit into a larger scheme bringing benefits to both themselves and to society.

Finally, following a Biblical framework of sexuality brings greater stability to society. AIDS, venereal disease, abortion, teen pregnancy, divorce, rape, and other tragedies are all the result of men and women moving beyond the perimeters of Biblical sexuality. Simple adherence to God's design for the sexes would virtually eliminate the destructive personal and social consequences just listed. Perhaps one of the best reasons for adhering to a Biblical view of sexuality is that it works for our benefit. It insures the greatest happiness and security for the individual and for society. It is our responsibility to articulate this view in a world floundering in sexual confusion.

The second challenge before us is that parents must reclaim the role of sex educator to their children. The most serious breakdown occurring in the area of our sexuality is happening where we would least expect—in the home. Research has shown that adolescents desire to learn the purpose of their sexuality from their parents; however, a survey of fourteen hundred parents found that less than 15 percent of mothers and 8 percent of fathers had ever talked to their children about sexual intercourse.[15]

So who is doing the job of teaching our children about sex? Peers, television, movies, pornography (the prime users of pornography are young people between the ages of twelve to seventeen), and of course the sex educators of our public schools. Is it any wonder every generation brings us closer to sexual chaos? Even if the sex education class at school taught only the basic facts of anatomy and biology (which it doesn't!), it would still have to be rejected because it would fail to teach our children the sanctity of sex or God's design for sex in their lives.

Sex education begins at home, and it is an eighteen-year course. To wait for the "big talk" will probably be too late. God gave parents the role of teaching and shaping their children's values, and the place of learning was in the home:

Hear, O Israel: The Lord our God, the Lord is one. Love the Lord your God with all your heart and with all your soul and with all your strength. These commandments that I give you today are to be upon your hearts. Impress them on your children. Talk about them when you sit at home and when you walk along the road, when you lie down and when you get up. (Deut. 6:4-7).

The responsibility to teach our children sexual values is ours as parents and it cannot be delegated, especially to those with a secular mindset. To do so will bring us a generation closer to the moral collapse of society. Changes must be made.

Fathers and mothers must begin spending more time with their children. Parents cannot influence the sexual values of their children if they do not spend time with them. A recent study of church parents and their children reported that the majority of teens spend less than thirty minutes a day with their fathers and 44 percent spend less than thirty minutes a day with their mothers.[16]

Fathers obviously cannot quit their jobs to spend time with their children, but mothers can and indeed they must. Yes, I am saying we must return to traditional sex roles. George Gilder is correct when he says that mothers are "the vessel of the ultimate values of the nation."[17]

The critical position of the woman in the home parallels her central position in all civilized society. Both derive from her necessary role in procreation and from the most primary and inviolable of human ties, the one between mother and child. In those extraordinary circumstances when this is broken . . . the group tends to sink to a totally bestial and amoral chaos.[18]

Is a career outside the home and the paucity of material benefits it brings really worth giving up the invaluable time mothers should be spending with their children, training them in the way they should go? Planned Parenthood would be more than happy to fill the void Christian parents are leaving in the area of sexual training.

The third challenge we must face if we are going to be effective agents of change in our world is that we must ultimately commit ourselves to what we believe. Mere intellectual assent to a particular set of values—even if they are Biblical—is not enough. Actions speak louder than words.

Unfortunately, many Christians see their Christianity as a private value that need not necessarily inform their behavior in the public sphere. Their attitude is reflected in the statement made by Ray Kroc, the founder of McDonald's hamburgers, who said, "I believe in God, the family and McDonald's—and in the office that order is reversed."[19] The result of this kind of mindset produces a kind of Christianity that social historian Theodore Roszak described as "privately engaging, but socially irrelevant."[20] Such a view is hardly what Jesus had in mind for His disciples when He called them to be salt and light in a darkened world (Matt. 5:13-17). For the Christian, the private and public spheres of life are not mutually exclusive of one another; indeed the two must be meshed together if cultural change is to take place. We must act on our convictions. Commitment always calls for a response to what we believe.

If we really believe that marriage is the basis of building strong families and strong societies, then we must commit ourselves to staying together. Surveys indicate that despite widespread agreement among Christians that divorce is detrimental to the family and society, Christians are every bit as likely as non-Christians to rely on divorce as an acceptable solution to a troubled marriage.[21] Somewhere we lost the meaning of vow and commitment, and our children and society are paying the price. Divorce should never be an option for those who belong to the community of reconciliation and forgiveness.

If we really believe that God has given us the responsibility to train our children in the way they should go, then we must commit ourselves to the task. It may mean getting along with less when Mom quits her job. It will mean pulling our children out of valueless sex education classes and perhaps the public school system altogether. Home schooling is not against the law (yet), and it will certainly be the surest way of instilling a Biblical worldview in our children.[22]

If we really believe our morals and values are being undermined by the secular elite of the television industry, then we must be committed to doing something about it. We cannot expect to fulfill our God-given responsibility of instilling Biblical values in our children by allowing them (or ourselves) to sit in indiscriminating silence for hours on end while themes of divorce, homosexuality, pre- and extramarital sex, and feminism challenge everything we believe about God's design and purpose for our sexuality. If the advertisers who are supporting television programming believe they can convince us in thirty seconds to buy their product, what can a program promoting a secular worldview accomplish in thirty minutes?

But what can we do? We can become more discriminating in our viewing and limit the time we spend watching. We can talk back. Never watch TV in silence. Question the values being presented out loud. Discuss them with your children. And when it gets too bad, simply turn the TV off . . . or throw it out. We can demand better programming and get it by going after the advertising sponsors whose advertising money makes the programming possible. Write letters to the sponsors and if they don't respond, boycott their products. Finally, we need those who can use their artistic and creative talents to infiltrate the industry and work to change it from within.

If we really believe that our politicians are indifferent to or wrongfully supportive of the issues of pornography, homosexuality, teenage abortion without parental consent, and other vital issues that affect our families and communities, then we must be committed enough to make ourselves heard. Your vote speaks loud and clear. Writing letters to your political representatives speaks volumes. It is said that every letter written, whether it is positive or negative, represents a thousand constituents—that is a lot of voices, and a lot of votes. Politicians listen to votes. And, contrary to popular belief, you *can* legislate morality. Although you cannot make people love what is right, you can make them do what is right. That is what the law is for (Rom. 13). Every law legislates morality by setting some standards for its citizens, and every citizen must ultimately make a moral decision to obey or disobey it.

If we really believe that pornography is a threat to our children and communities, then we must commit ourselves to fighting it with all the time, effort, and resources available to us. The Christian community must become better informed about this issue. Following this chapter, a brief list of books and antipornography organizations is provided to inform you about the real nature of the problem and what can be done about it. Be committed enough to read a book or write one of the organizations for further information.

For the Christian community to be truly effective in changing the world, we must be committed to the ideal that everyone can make a significant impact. For most of us it will start right where we are, shaping our families and our own communities. Nehemiah recognized this principle in rebuilding the walls of Jerusalem when he instructed the priests to carry out the repairs ". . . each in front of his own house" (Neh. 3:28). Rebuilding the ruins of sexuality in our culture will take some time; so the time to start is now. Hopefully it will be said of our generation what was said of the men of Issachar, ". . . who understood the times and knew what they should do" (1 Chron. 12:32).

ANTI-PORNOGRAPHY RESOURCES

Books
Pornography, A Human Tragedy, Tom Minnery, editor (Wheaton: Tyndale House, 1986).
Donald Wildmon, *The Case Against Pornography* (Wheaton: Victor Books, 1986).

Organizations
Citizens for Decency Through Law
2331 West Royal Palm Road, Suite 105
Phoenix, Arizona 85021
(602) 995-2600

Morality in Media
475 Riverside Drive
New York, New York 10115
(212) 870-3222

The National Coalition Against Pornography
800 Compton Road, Suite 9248
Cincinnati, Ohio 45231
(513) 521-NCAP

The National Federation for Decency
P.O. Drawer 2440
Tupelo, Mississippi 38803
(800) 322-3624

NOTES

CHAPTER ONE: PURPOSE IN POLARITY
1. Margaret Mead, *Male and Female: A Study of the Sexes in a Changing World* (New York: Morrow, 1949), p. 173, quoted in George Gilder, *Sexual Suicide* (New York: Quadrangle/The New York Times Book Company, 1973), p. 59.
2. Francis Schaeffer, *Back to Freedom and Dignity* (Downers Grove, IL: InterVarsity Press, 1972), p. 25.
3. Karl Barth was the first major theologian to adopt this position in his *Church Dogmatics III*. For two modern approaches to this position, but which come to different conclusions, see Paul Jewett, *Man As Male and Female* (Grand Rapids, MI: Wm. B. Eerdmans, 1975), and Ray Anderson, *On Being Human: Essays in Theological Anthropology* (Grand Rapids, MI: Wm. B. Eerdmans, 1982).
4. J. I. Packer, *Knowing Man* (Westchester, IL: Crossway Books, 1978), p. 30.
5. While the doctrine of the Trinity contains more than we can understand, I do affirm traditional Biblical theology which states that God is one in three distinct persons.
6. Jewett, *Man As Male and Female*, p. 36.
7. Anderson, *On Being Human*, p. 51.
8. *Ibid.*, p. 114.
9. George Carey, *I Believe in Man* (Grand Rapids, MI: Wm. B. Eerdmans, 1977), p. 149.
10. Anderson, *On Being Human*, p. 116.
11. Lloyd Saxton, *The Individual, Marriage, and the Family* (Belmont, CA: Wadsworth Publishing Co., 1986), p. 149.
12. Anderson, *On Being Human*, p. 106.

CHAPTER TWO: MARRIAGE—MANDATE OR OPTION?
1. Jacques Monod, quoted in Schaeffer, *Back to Freedom and Dignity*, p. 11.
2. Jacquelin R. Kasun, "The Population Bomb Threat: A Look at the Facts," quoted in Mary Pride, *The Way Home* (Westchester, IL: Crossway Books, 1985), p. 60.

3. George Gilder, *Men and Marriage* (Gretna, LA: Pelican, 1986), p. 174.

4. Artur Weiser, "The Psalms," *The Old Testament Library* (Philadelphia: Westminster Press, 1962), p. 144.

5. Bronislaw Malinowski, *Marriage: Past and Present,* as quoted in Gilder, *Men and Marriage,* p. 15.

6. Mary Pride in her book *The Way Home* makes the strongest case for this position. See especially Chapters 4, 5, and 6.

7. James Dobson, *Dr. Dobson Answers Your Questions About Marriage & Sexuality* (Wheaton, IL: Tyndale House, 1982), p. 44.

8. "One-Parent Families Still Increasing," *Youthworker Update,* Vol. 1, No. 6, Feb. 1987.

9. *Ibid.*

10. 1986 Bureau of Justice Statistics Bulletin figures found in *Youthworker Update,* Vol. 1, No. 7, March 1987.

11. George Carey, *I Believe in Man,* p. 153.

12. James Dobson, "A New Look At Masculinity and Femininity," booklet published by Focus on the Family, Pomona, CA, 1985, p. 8.

13. George Gilder, *Sexual Suicide,* p. 6.

CHAPTER THREE: THE ROAD TO DESTRUCTION

1. For a discussion of the Supreme Court's definition of obscenity, see Chapter Seven.

2. John H. Gagnon, *Human Sexuality, An Age of Ambiguity* (Boston: Little, Brown and Co., 1975), p. 64.

3. *Ibid.*

4. *Ibid.*

5. John Murray, "The Epistle to the Romans," *The New International Commentary on the New Testament* (Grand Rapids, MI: Wm. B. Eerdmans, 1959), p. 47.

6. Pride, *The Way Home,* p. 28.

CHAPTER FOUR: FEMINISM

1. For insights into feminist demeanor see Joan Cassell, *A Group Called Women, Sisterhood and Symbolism in the Feminist Movement* (New York: David McKay Co., Inc., 1977), p. 82ff.

2. "The Myth of Post Feminism," *Ms.,* June 1986, p. 30.

3. Mary Pride, *The Way Home,* p. xi.

4. Mary Daly, *The Church and the Second Sex* (Boston: Beacon Press, 1985), p. xxv.

5. Beverly Harrison, *Making The Connections, Essays in Feminist Social Ethics,* ed. Carol Robb (Boston: Beacon Press, 1985), p. 7.

6. Betty Friedan, *The Feminine Mystique* (New York: Parquin Books, 1965), pp. 292, 293.

7. Shulamith Firestone, *The Dialectic of Sex* (New York: William Morrow and Co., 1970), p. 8ff.

8. *Ibid.,* p. 11ff.

9. *Ibid.,* pp. 233-236.

10. Kate Millett, *Sexual Politics* (Garden City, NY: Doubleday and Co., Inc., 1970), p. 62.

11. *Ibid.*
12. Simone de Beauvoir, quoted in Daly, *The Church and the Second Sex*, p. 53.
13. Judith A. Dorney, "Religious Education and the Development of Young Women," in *Women's Issues in Religious Education*, ed. Fern Giltner (Birmingham, AL: Religious Education Press, 1985), p. 49. Here Dorney is quoting Letty Russell.
14. Daly, *The Church and the Second Sex*, p. xvi.
15. Daly, "Theology After the Demise Of God the Father: A Call for the Castration of Sexist Religion," *Sexist Religion and Women in the Church*, ed. Alice Hageman (New York: Association Press, 1974), pp. 132, 138, 139. Quoted in Pride, *The Way Home*, p. 8.
16. Naomi Goldenberg, *Changing of the Gods, Feminism and the End of Traditional Religions* (Boston: Beacon Press, 1979), p. 103.
17. *Ibid.*, p. 22
18. Beverly Wildung Harrison, *Making the Connections, Essays in Feminist Social Ethics*, p. 38.
19. *Ibid.*, p. 22ff.
20. Quoted in Rosemary Radford Ruether, *Women—Church: Theology and Practice of Feminist Liturgical Communities* (San Francisco: Harper & Row, 1985), p. 135.
21. Peggy Ann Way, quoted in Goldenberg, *Changing of the Gods*, p. 23.
22. Letty Russell, *Human Liberation in a Feminist Perspective—A Theology* (Philadelphia: Westminster Press, 1974), p. 51.
23. *Feminist Interpretaton of the Bible*, ed. Letty M. Russell (Philadelphia: Westminster Press, 1985), Chapters 9, 10.
24. Denise Lardner Carmody, *Feminism and Christianity, A Two-Way Reflection* (Nashville: Abingdon, 1982), p. 91.
25. Ruether, *Women—Church*, p. 136.
26. *Ibid.*, p. 132.
27. Goldenberg, *Changing of the Gods*, p. 9.
28. Pride, *The Way Home*, p. 7.
29. Anne Carson, *Feminist Spirituality and the Feminine Divine* (Trumansburg, NY: The Crossing Press, 1986).
30. James R. Edwards, "Does God Really Want to be Called 'Father'? How We Refer to God Makes A Difference," *Christianity Today*, Vol. 30, Feb. 21, 1986, p. 28.
31. Sally Binford, "Are Goddesses and Martriarchies Merely Figments of Feminist Imagination?," in *The Politics of Women's Spirituality*, ed. Charlene Spretnak (Garden City, NY: Anchor Books, 1982), pp. 541, 542.
32. Goldenberg, *Changing of the Gods*, p. 92 as quoted in Pride, *The Way Home*, p. 5.
33. *Ibid.*, pp. 93, 94.
34. Carson, *Feminist Spirituality and the Feminist Divine*, p. 3.
35. Goldenberg, *Changing of the Gods*, p. 91.
36. Joan Cassell, *A Group Called Women*, p. 93.
37. Harrison, *Making the Connections*, p. xvi.
38. *Ibid.*, pp. xix, 2, 29.

39. Shulamith Firestone, "Love" in Cassell, *A Group Called Women,* p. 71.
40. William O'Neill, "Feminism as a Radical Ideology," in *Dissent: Explorations in the History of American Radicalism,* ed. Alfred Young (Dekalb, IL: Northern Illinois University Press, 1968), p. 298.
41. *Ibid.*
42. Simone de Beauvoir, quoted in John Charvet, *Feminism* (London: J. M. Dent and Sons Ltd., 1982), p. 106.
43. Eva Figes, quoted in *ibid.,* p. 110.
44. Germaine Greer, quoted in *ibid.,* p. 116.
45. Quoted in Cassell, *A Group Called Women,* p. 68.
46. *Ibid.,* p. 64.
47. B. Ehrenreich, E. Hess, and G. Jacobs, "Re-making Love, the Real Sexual Revolution," *Ms.,* July 1986, p. 42.
48. Ann Koedt, "The Myth of the Vaginal Orgasm," in *Notes from the Second Year: Women's Liberation* (New York: Radical Feminists, 1970), p. 41.
49. Ehreinreich, Hess, Jacobs, "Re-making Love," p. 40ff.
50. *Ibid.,* p. 82.
51. *Ibid.*
52. Alexandra Penney, "What About Sex?," *Ms.,* June 1985, p. 94.
53. Cassell, *A Group Called Women,* p. 76.
54. *Ibid.,* p. 72.
55. *Ibid.,* p. 79.
56. *Ibid.,* p. 80.
57. Martha Shelley, "Notes of a Radical Lesbian," in *Sisterhood Is Powerful: An Anthology of Writing from the Women's Liberation Movement,* ed. Robin Morgan (New York: Vintage, 1970), p. 307.
58. Quoted in Cassell, *A Group Called Women,* p. 184.
59. Simone de Beauvoir, quoted in Charvet, *Feminism,* p. 107.
60. Amanda Spake, "The Propaganda War Over Abortion," *Ms.,* July 1985, p. 91.

CHAPTER FIVE: HOMOSEXUALITY

1. There are eight references to homosexuality in Scripture, and in all eight it is condemned as sin. See Gen. 19:1-11; Lev. 18:22; 20:13; Deut. 23:17; Judg. 19:22-25; Rom. 1:26, 27; 1 Cor. 6:9, 10; 1 Tim. 1:9, 10.
2. G. C. Berkouwer, "Sin," *Studies in Dogmatics,* trans. Philip Holtrop (Grand Rapids: Wm. B. Eerdmans, 1971), p. 286.
3. For a fuller treatment of the Reformers' view of sin, especially in comparison to the Roman theology of venial and mortal sin, see *ibid.,* p. 302ff.
4. William P. Wilson, "Biology, Psychology, and Homosexuality," *What You Should Know About Homosexuality,* ed. Charles Keysor (Grand Rapids: Zondervan, 1979), p. 160.
5. George Gilder, *Men and Marriage,* p. 62.
6. Tim LaHaye, *What Everyone Should Know About Homosexuality* (Wheaton, IL: Living Books, Tyndale House, 1985), p. 47.
7. *Ibid.*
8. Wilson, "Biology, Psychology and Homosexuality," p. 158.
9. Gilder, *Men and Marriage,* p. 73.

10. "AIDS: At the Dawn of Fear," *U.S. News & World Report*, Jan. 12, 1987, p. 62.
11. Wilson, "Biology, Psychology, and Homosexuality," pp. 151-154.
12. C. A. Tripp, *The Homosexual Matrix* (New York: New American Library, 1975), p. 77.
13. David F. Busby, "Sexual Deviations—A Psychiatric Overview," in *Proceeding of the Fourteenth Annual Convention of the Christian Association for Psychological Studies*, April 1967, pp. 55-60. Quoted from Wm. H. McKain, Jr., "Ministry and Homosexuality," in *What You Should Know About Homosexuality*, p. 204.
14. Clyde M. Narramore, *Encyclopedia of Psychological Problems* (Grand Rapids: Zondervan, 1966), p. 114.
15. *Ibid.*
16. Wm. H. McKain, Jr., "Ministry and Homosexuality," p. 205.
17. Leanne Payne, *The Healing of the Homosexual* (Westchester, IL: Crossway Books, 1985), p. 2ff.
18. Gilder, *Men and Marriage*, p. 71.
19. *Ibid.*
20. Victor Cline, "Effects of Pornography on Behavior," *Bible Advocate*, Jan. 1985, p. 9.
21. Enrique Rueda, *The Homosexual Network, Private Lives and Public Policy* (Old Greenwich, CT: The Devin Adair Co., 1982), p. 3.
22. *Ibid.*, p. 470.
23. For an excellent critique on the acceptability of homosexuality in the U.S., see *ibid.*, pp. 3-28.
24. *Ibid.*, p. 198.
25. *America*, Nov. 19, 1977. Quoted from *ibid.*
26. *Ibid.*, pp. 202, 203.
27. David Thorstad, "A Statement to the Gay Liberation Movement on the Issue of Man/Boy Love," *Gay Community News*, Jan. 6, 1979, p. 5. Quoted in *ibid.*, p. 203.
28. Quoted in *ibid.*, pp. 87, 88.
29. Quoted in *Biblical Principles Concerning Issues of Importance to Godly Christians* (Plymouth, MA: Plymouth Rock Foundation, 1984), p. 271.
30. Eric Johnson, *Sex: Telling It Straight* (Lippincolt, 1979), quoted in Rueda, *The Homosexual Network*, p. 19.
31. Quoted in Rueda, *The Homosexual Network*, p. 19.
32. *Ibid.*, p. 117.
33. *Ibid.*
34. *Ibid.*, p. 93.
35. Quoted in *ibid.*, p. 221.
36. Charles E. Rice, "Nature's Intolerance of Abuse," *The Wanderer*, Aug. 6, 1981, quoted in *ibid.*, p. 91.

CHAPTER SIX: ANDROGYNY
1. G. Diliberto, "Invasion of the Gender Benders," *People Weekly*, 21:96-99, April 23, 1984, p. 96.
2. For a thorough history of androgyny in the music industry, see Steve

Simels, *Gender Chameleons: Androgyny in Rock and Roll* (New York: Timbre Books/Arbor House Publishing Co., 1985).

3. "Gender Benders; The Year of Living Androgynously," *Life,* Jan. 1985, p. 94 (6).

4. John Leo, "The Eleventh Megatrend: Ralph and Wanda Grapple with Boy George and Androgyny," *Time,* July 23, 1984, p. 104.

5. James Dobson, "A New Look at Masculinity and Femininity," Focus on the Family, 1985, p. 4ff. Excerpted from James Dobson, *Straight Talk to Men* and *Their Wives* (Waco, TX: Word, 1980).

6. James Levine, *Psychology Today,* Nov. 1979, Vol. 13, No. 6, p. 147. Quoted in *ibid.,* p. 5.

7. George Gilder, *Men and Marriage,* p. ix.

8. *Ibid.,* pp. ix, x.

9. Quoted in the Tacoma *News Tribune,* Jan. 12, 1986.

10. Anne Hollander, "Dressed to Thrill: The Cool and Casual Style of the New American Androgyny," *New Republic,* Jan. 28, 1985, p. 28.

11. Liza Dalby, "Yes Ma'am, A Woman Can be More Like a Man!," *Cosmopolitan,* Vol. 200, Jan. 1986, p. 200.

12. Quoted in "Gender Benders," *Life,* p. 96.

13. Quoted in G. Diliberto, "Invasion of the Gender Benders," *People Weekly,* Vol. 21, April 23, 1984, p. 99.

14. Carole Wade Offir, *Human Sexuality* (New York: Harcourt, Brace, Jovanovich, Inc., 1982), p. 26.

15. Ellen Piel Cook, *Psychological Androgyny* (New York: Pergamon Press, 1985), pp. 24, 34.

16. June Singer, *Androgyny, Toward a New Theory of Sexuality* (Garden City, NY: Anchor Press/Doubleday, 1976), p. 276.

17. *Ibid.,* pp. 22, 35.

18. *Ibid.,* p. 294.

19. Alexandra G. Kaplan and Mary Anne Sedney, *Psychology and Sex Roles, An Androgynous Perspective* (Boston: Little, Brown and Co., 1980), p. 79.

20. *Ibid.*

21. Robert G. Pielke, "Are Androgyny and Sexuality Compatible?," in *Femininity, Masculinity, and Androgyny,* ed. Mary Vetterling (Totowa, NJ: Braggin, Dowman and Littlefield, 1982), p. 188.

22. Mary Anne Warren, "Is Androgyny the Answer to Sexual Stereotyping?" in *ibid.,* p. 181.

23. *Ibid.*

24. Joyce Trebilcot, "Two Forms of Androgynism," in *ibid.,* p. 164.

25. *Ibid.*

26. Robert G. Pielke, "Are Androgyny and Sexuality Compatible?," in *ibid.,* p. 194.

27. June Singer, *Androgyny, Toward a New Theory of Sexuality,* p. 30.

28. Ellen Piel Cook, *Psychological Androgyny,* p. 21.

29. Mary Anne Warren, "Is Adrogyny the Answer to Sexual Stereotyping?" p. 180.

30. June Singer, *Androgyny, Toward a New Theory of Sexuality,* p. 305.

31. *Ibid.,* p. 306.
32. *Ibid.,* p. 305.

CHAPTER SEVEN: PORNOGRAPHY

1. This description was taken from a detailed synopsis of *Lisa, 10 Years, and Her Dog* found in *Final Report of the Attorney General's Commission on Pornography* (Nashville: Rutledge Hill Press, 1986), pp. 431, 432.
2. *Final Report of the Attorney General's Commission on Pornography,* pp. 17, 18.
3. See the research of Judith Reisman contained in "How Pornography Changes Attitudes" by David A. Scott in *Pornography. A Human Tragedy,* ed. Tom Minnery (Wheaton, IL: Tyndale House Publishers, Inc., 1986), p. 136.
4. David A. Scott, "How Pornography Changes Attitudes," in *Pornography. A Human Tragedy,* p. 136.
5. Donald Wildmon, *The Case Against Pornography* (Wheaton, IL: Victor Books, 1986), p. 11.
6. *Final Report of the Attorney General's Commission on Pornography,* p. xii.
7. *Ibid.*
8. *Ibid.,* p. 366.
9. *Ibid.,* p. 365.
10. James Dobson, "Enough Is Enough," in *Pornography. A Human Tragedy,* p. 35.
11. *Ibid.,* p. 36.
12. David A. Scott, "How Pornography Changes Attitudes," in *Pornography. A Human Tragedy,* p. 116.
13. These "categories" or "classes" of material can be found in the Commission's report beginning at p. 39ff. For a briefer overview, a summary is provided in the introduction by Michael McManus, pp. xix, xx.
14. David A. Scott, "How Pornography Changes Attitudes," in *Pornography. A Human Tragedy,* p. 135.
15. *Ibid.*
16. Donald Wildmon, *The Case Against Pornography,* p. 61.
17. *Ibid.,* p. 62.
18. David Scott, "How Pornography Changes Attitudes," p. 121.
19. Dolf Zillmann, *Proceedings of the Symposium on Media Violence and Pornography* (Toronto: Media Action Group, 1984), p. 96. Quoted in Scott, "How Pornography Changes Attitudes," p. 121.
20. David S. Scott, "How Pornography Changes Attitudes," p. 119.
21. *Ibid.,* p. 139.
22. *Ibid.,* p. 141.
23. John H. Court, *Pornography: A Christian Critique* (Downers Grove, IL: InterVarsity Press, 1980), p. 81.
24. James Dobson, "Enough Is Enough," p. 40.
25. For the pornographic lyrical content of some of today's most popular songs, see Appendix Two, "Pornography Rock Lyrics," in *Pornography: A Human Tragedy,* pp. 335ff.—or your local record store.

26. James Dobson, "Enough Is Enough," p. 43.

27. Lynn Hirschberg, "Giving Good Phone," *Rolling Stone Yearbook*, 1983, p. 141. Quoted in Bob Maddux, *Fantasy Explosion* (Ventura, CA: Regal Books, 1986), p. 33.

CHAPTER EIGHT: MASTURBATION

1. Quoted in Carole Wade Offir, *Human Sexuality* (New York: Harcourt Brace Jovanovich, Inc., 1982), p. 17.

2. *Ibid.*, p. 190.

3. *Ibid.*

4. *Ibid.*, p. 91.

5. Donald Goergen in *The Sexual Celibate* (Minneapolis: Seabury Press, 1947), p. 199, 200. Quoted in Joyce Huggett, *Dating, Sex and Friendship* (Downers Grove, IL: InterVarsity Press, 1985), p. 163.

6. Herbert J. Miles, *Sexual Understanding Before Marriage* (Grand Rapids: Zondervan Publishing House, 1971), pp. 145-150.

7. Joyce Haggett, *Dating, Sex and Friendship*, p. 164.

8. A. C. Kinsey, W. B. Pomeroy, and C. E. Martin, *Sexual Behaviour in the Human Male* (Philadelphia: W. B. Sanders, 1948).

9. James L. McCary, *McCary's Human Sexuality*, 3rd. ed. (New York: D. Van Nostrand, 1978), p. 150.

10. Clyde M. Narramore, *Encyclopedia of Psychological Problems* (Grand Rapids: Zondervan Publishing House, 1966), pp. 157, 159.

11. Kinsey, *Sexual Behaviour in the Human Male*.

12. Offir, *Human Sexuality*, p. 187.

13. Miles, *Sexual Understanding Before Marriage*, p. 147.

14. June Singer, *Androgyny, Toward a New Theory of Sexuality* (Garden City, NY: Anchor Press/Doubleday, 1976), pp. 300, 305, 306.

CHAPTER NINE: THE LAST TABOOS

1. See John Gagnon, *Human Sexualities* (Glenview, IL: Scott Foresman, 1977).

2. J. Money, *Paraphilias,* in eds. J. Money and H. Musaph, *Handbook of Sexuality* (North Holland, Amsterdam: El Sevier, 1977), pp. 917-928. Described in Carole Wade Offir, *Human Sexuality*, p. 248.

3. Statistics quoted from Angela R. Carl, *Child Abuse: What You Can Do About It* (Cincinnati: Standard Publishing, 1985), p. 31.

4. Quoted in Elizabeth Stark, "Views of Child Molesters," *Psychology Today*, April 1, 1985, p. 8.

5. Anne H. Rosenfeld, "Discovering and Dealing with Deviant Sex," *Psychology Today*, April 1985, p. 8.

6. *Ibid.*, p. 10.

7. *Ibid.*

8. Offir, *Human Sexuality*, p. 187. Offir notes that sexual fantasies typically involve some sort of forbidden behavior.

9. *Ibid.*, p. 248.

10. Dr. Vince Huntington, quoted on Stanley Tonight, KUSI, Channel 51, San Diego, May 15, 1987.

11. "Ask Dr. Ruth," in the *San Diego Union*, June 10, 1987.
12. *Rolling Stone*, Feb. 2, 1984, p. 28.
13. *Ibid.*, p. 250.
14. Clyde Narramore, *Encyclopedia of Psychological Problems*, p. 213.
15. Quoted in Offir, *Human Sexuality*, p. 252.
16. *Ibid.*
17. *Ibid.*, p. 254.
18. *Ibid.*
19. Narramore, *Encyclopedia of Psychological Problems*, p. 213.
19. Offir, *Human Sexuality*, p. 258.
20. Narramore, *Encyclopedia of Psychological Problems*, p. 214.
21. Offir, *Human Sexuality*, p. 260.

CHAPTER TEN: REBUILDING THE RUINS
1. Earl D. Wilson, *Sexual Sanity, Breaking Free from Uncontrolled Habits* (Downers Grove, IL: InterVarsity Press, 1984), p. 36.
2. *Ibid.*, p. 37.
3. *Ibid.*, p. 52.
4. *Ibid.*
5. *Ibid.*, p. 53, 54.
6. For a fuller explanation of the conscience and how it operates, see Jack V. Rozell, "Implications of the New Testament Concept of Conscience for Pastoral Counseling," in *Biblical and Psychological Perspectives for Christian Counselors*, ed. Robert K. Bower (Pasadena, CA: Publishers Services of the William Carey Library, 1974).
7. Anderson, *On Being Human, Essays in Theological Anthropology*, p. 126.
8. W. H. Lewis, ed., *Letters of C. S. Lewis* (New York: Harcourt, Brace, Jovanovich, 1966), p. 189.

CHAPTER ELEVEN: REBUILDING THE RUINS IN SOCIETY
1. Arnold Toynbee, *A Study of History*, Vol. IV (London: Oxford University Press, 1939), p. 120.
2. See Carl Wilson, *Our Dance Has Turned to Death* (Atlanta: Renewal Publishing Co., 1979).
3. This is the view promoted by feminist Betty Dodson on the "Phil Donahue Show" aired on NBC, December 1, 1987.
4. Ron Reagan on a PBS special, "Changing the Rules," aired November 6, 1987, Channel 15, San Diego. During this same program, musician Ruben Blades demonstrates how to use a condom using a banana as a prop.
5. Judith Reisman, "Thirty-six Children Sample Cartoons and Photographs from *Playboy, Penthouse,* and *Hustler* with Accompanying Analysis," The Institute for Media Education, 1987.
6. Figures reported in Marlin Maddoux, "Deception in the Media" in *Judgment in the Gate*, ed. Richie Martin (Westchester, IL: Crossway Books, 1986), p. 148.
7. L. Lichter, S. Lichter, and S. Rothman, "Hollywood and America: The Odd Couple," *Public Opinion*, January 1983, pp. 54-58, cited in G. Burna

and W. P. McKay, *Vital Signs* (Westchester, IL: Crossway Books, 1984), pp. 56, 57.

8. See Jacqueline Kasun, "The Truth About Sex Education" in *School Based Clinics,* ed. B. Mosbacker (Westchester, IL: Crossway Books, 1987), p. 29ff. Also, Sandalyn McKasson, "Sex and Seduction in the Classroom" in *Judgment in the Gate,* p. 90ff.

9. Barrett Mosbacker, "The Final Step: Clinics, Children and Contraceptives" in *School Based Clinics,* p. 63ff.

10. "Morality," *U.S. News and World Report,* December 9, 1985, pp. 52, 53.

11. "New Strains in Dixie's Bible Belt," *ibid.,* p. 59.

12. These prinicples have been articulated in Barrett Mosbacker, "The Christian, Morality, and Public Policy" in *School Based Clinics,* pp. 186, 187.

13. *Ibid.,* p. 187.

14. *Ibid.,* p. 190.

15. E. Roberts, D. Kline, and J. Gagnon, *Family Life and Sexual Learning of Children,* Vol. 1 (Cambridge, MA: Population Education, Inc., 1981), p. 29 found in Josh McDowell and Dick Day, *Why Wait?* (San Bernardino: Here's Life Publishers, 1987), p. 379.

16. Merton Strommen and A. Irene Strommen, *Five Cries of Parents* (San Francisco: Harper & Row, 1985), p. 79, found in McDowell, *Why Wait?,* p. 386.

17. George Gilder, *Men and Marriage,* p. 169.

18. *Ibid.,* p. 168.

19. Quoted in *Context,* November 15, 1981, p. 6, quoted in Os Guinness, *The Gravedigger File* (Downers Grove, IL: InterVarsity Press, 1983), p. 63.

20. Theodore Roszak, *Where the Wasteland Ends* (New York: Doubleday, 1973), p. 449, quoted in Guinness, *The Gravedigger File,* p. 79.

21. George Barna and William McKay, *Vital Signs: Emerging Social Trends and the Future of American Christianity,* pp. 11-13.

22. For an excellent treatment on this subject see Mary Pride, *The Way Home* (Westchester, IL: Crossway Books, 1985).

INDEX